Joy • Peace • Patience

Kindness • Goodness

Faithfulness • Gentleness

Self-Control

ECHOES OF HEAVEN

Mark E. Jones

HEARTSPRING PUBLISHING · JOPLIN, MISSOURI

To My Wife Gail . . .
You have consistently conveyed
the fruit of God's Spirit
to me–
especially love.

HeartSpring Publishing
On the web at www.heartspringpublishing.com
Toll-free order line 1-800-289-3300
A division of College Press Publishing Co.
www.collegepress.com

Cover design by Brett Lyerla

Photos are the author's own

International Standard Book Number 0-89900-920-4

CONTENTS

2000 AND BEYOND STUDIES FOR SMALL GROUPS

In pursuit of our stated goal, "Every Christian a Bible Student," College Press has, since 1995, been publishing a series of *Studies for Small Groups*, which now fall under our HeartSpring imprint. These have proved very popular, both for group and individual study on a variety of topics and Scripture texts. Although, with the year 2000, we have changed the outward appearance of these study booklets, our commitment is still to providing solid, thought-provoking studies that will make a life-changing difference in the reader.

Of course, although we call these studies "for small groups," they are equally suited for individual study. If you are simply reading the book for your own benefit, please do take the time to use the "Reflecting on . . ." questions to focus your own thoughts. In a small group study, the questions should not only be used as a review, to see if you remember what was actually said in that lesson by the writer, but to help spark discussion of the further *implications* of the lesson material. Nor should you consider the questions that are provided the only questions to be asked. Any study is only as good as the effort you put into it, and the group leader should have read the lesson through thoroughly before the class meets, as well as encouraging all other members of the group to do so if possible. If the leader has gone through the lesson in advance, he or she will probably have thought of other questions, some of which may never have even occurred to the writer or editors of the study. After all, what is important is not just the bare facts of the lesson, but how they intersect with your own path in the Christian walk.

Above all, do not feel you have to race through the lessons. Although the number of lessons is purposely kept small so that no one has to commit in advance to an endless period of time on the study, you should not cut off discussion of an important issue just to fit the whole of the lesson into one study session. Nor do you want to leave off the end of a lesson because you didn't get it all in during the allotted time. The greatest advantage of the small group setting is the flexibility you have, allowing you to carry over discussion to the next session. Take full advantage of this flexibility.

ECHOES OF HEAVEN

Of all the new cartoons that have come out in recent years, my kids and I enjoy *Johnny Bravo* the best. Johnny is a handsome and muscular but really dumb guy who talks like Elvis and thinks he's God's gift to the world. In one episode, Johnny stands on top of a cliff and shouts across a canyon, "I'm pretty." To his surprise, a voice answers back, "I'm pretty." Unimpressed, Johnny yells a little louder, "No, I am." The voice counters, "No, I am." Somewhat taken aback by the arrogance of this other voice, Johnny shouts even louder, "I'm prettier." The voice responds, "I'm prettier." Clearly frustrated by now, Johnny insists, "You're ugly," and the voice comes back, "You're ugly." At this point Johnny changes tactics and hollers, "I know you are, but what am I?" and the voice echoes, "I know you are, but what am I?" Johnny finally gives in and admits, "Man, *he's* good!"

You have likely been in a situation where conditions were just right for your voice to echo. Or perhaps you have listened to music in a concert hall, and, as the last note was played, the final crescendo reverberated through the auditorium. It's only natural. An echo is the repetition of sound caused by a reflection of sound waves: when conditions are right, an echo is unavoidable. The key to remember is that you cannot have an echo without an original sound, just as you cannot have a reflection in a mirror without an original image. An echo is always the by-product of something else.

The Apostle Paul suggests that when the Holy Spirit lives inside of us, certain character traits become inevitable. These traits—known as the Fruit of the Spirit—originate with God Himself and then *echo* throughout our lives. In fact, as Christians, these traits—this fruit—should continue to expand in us as we mature. But how can we be sure that happens? How can we reflect the attributes of God in our daily lives? We follow the example of Jesus. After all, isn't that the goal of every Christian: to become like Jesus, to possess His heart, His mind, His emotions? Consider Paul's summary of this concept in Galatians 5:22-23, "The fruit of the Spirit is love, joy, peace, patience, kindness, goodness, faithfulness, gentleness and self-control. Against such things there is no law." Nobody writes laws against traits such as these. As we cultivate these traits through the power of God's Spirit, we will find that our lives echo the sounds—the music—the harmony of heaven.

Consider this:

Life often throws monkey wrenches into the works of daily living. We think we have everything under control, but then we discover our spouse has blown all our money on gambling, or our teenager gets involved with drugs, or our three-year-old throws a temper tantrum. In circumstances such as these finding the will or heart to love the other person can be a struggle. In similar life situations where do you look to find the strength for love and forgiveness? Be prepared to share your thoughts.

1

ECHOING GOD'S LOVE

In this lesson:

- Defining love
- An example of how Jesus loved others
- Character traits of love

The fruit of the Spirit—the *product* of God's Holy Spirit living inside of us—is first of all love. Frankly, I don't think there is any characteristic which defines Jesus more completely than this one. But what exactly is love? We hear a lot about it in our culture, but I wonder if we really know what it is. People say things like, "Love is never having to say you're sorry." "Love makes the world go round." "Love is like the chicken pox; everybody catches it sometime." We talk about "falling in love," "staying in love," "making love." Then there are the bumper stickers with the big red hearts on them: "I Love Skydiving," "I Love Terre Haute," "I Love Country Music." I grew up in Louisville, Kentucky, and attended Male High School. It had been an all-boy's school in decades past, and the name was never changed. Our mascot was the bulldog. When a friend of mine moved to Louisville several years ago, never having heard of Male High School, you can imagine how shocked he was to see a bumper sticker which said, "I Love Male Bulldogs!" That was *way more* information than he needed to know!

What is love? Is it simply an emotional feeling, something we "fall into" or even "fall out of"? Is it a matter of the head or of the heart, the mind or the emotions? The dictionary uses words like "affection," "attraction," "warm attachment," but even those are a little vague. The Apostle Paul describes love in 1 Corinthians 13:4-8a, "Love is patient, love is kind. It does not envy, it does not boast, it is not proud. It is not rude, it is not self-seeking, it is not easily angered, it keeps no record of wrongs. Love does not delight in evil but rejoices with the truth. It always protects, always trusts, always hopes, always perseveres. Love never fails." Interestingly, he uses more words telling us what love is *not* than what love is.

Jesus said in John 13:34, "A new command I give you: Love one another. *As I have loved you*, so you must love one another." Now, if that's the case—that we are to love as Jesus did—then it seems obvious that true love, whatever it is, ought to look like Jesus. Suddenly, new words come to mind like "servanthood" and "sacrifice" and "vulnerability" and "unselfishness" and even "suffering." That doesn't sound much at all like the love we see on

True love, whatever it is, ought to look like Jesus.

TV and in the movies, but that is what Jesus modeled. The attention He showed to the woman at the well, the second chance He offered the woman caught in adultery, the compassion that He felt for the rich young ruler, the hope that He granted the thief on the cross, the love that He expressed as He gave His life show that Jesus is all about love.

Why is Jesus' kind of love such a challenge in our culture? For one thing, society's view of love is so often misguided. People think sex is love, but then their bodies begin to age or the thrill of a new conquest wears off, and many who thought they were loved find themselves brokenhearted and alone. Parents think indulging their children with every toy and luxury imaginable is the ultimate expression of love, but how many kids are left spoiled and alone while mom and dad spend countless hours working overtime to pay the bills? And once those kids grow up, they find out that the unrealistic expectations their parents built into them can no longer be met. Their spouses and their employers and their friends don't respond to their every whim. They discover they were bought off by parents who mistakenly equated possessions with affection.

Perhaps most tragic of all, love is often simply absent. Second Timothy 3:1-3a says, "There will be terrible times in the last days. People will be lovers of themselves, lovers of money, boastful, proud, abusive, disobedient to their parents, ungrateful, unholy, *without love*." We have all watched the news in horror, listening to reports of suicide bombers, child abductions, rape, and murder, wondering how on earth anyone could be so evil—so consumed with hatred. We hear reports of abuse such as husbands beating their wives, parents exploiting their children, child molesters doing irreparable damage to students, neighbors, and strangers. We read articles about caregivers who steal from the elderly, gangs who murder their rivals, drug pushers who turn children into addicts. And beyond those who aggressively bring harm, the fact is, many of us selfishly live for ourselves and ignore the needs of those around us. It's not that we would ever hurt anyone intentionally, but we simply neglect opportunities to reach out to people in a positive way. "The fruit of the Spirit is love." What exactly does that mean? It has long been said that "a picture is worth a thousand words." Maybe the best way to define love is to look at a snapshot from the life of Jesus.

A WOMAN IN TROUBLE

In John chapter 8, we find Jesus facing an awkward dilemma. The religious leaders, the so-called spiritual giants of Israel, had dragged a woman before Him. "Israel's finest" normally would not have given her the time of day, but we'll see that Jesus gave her the most important day of her life. Beginning in verse 1,

> Jesus went to the Mount of Olives. At dawn he appeared again in the temple courts, where all the people gathered around him, and he sat down to teach them. The teachers of the law and the Pharisees brought in a woman caught in adultery. They made her stand before the group and said to Jesus, "Teacher, this woman was caught in the act of adultery. In the Law Moses commanded us to stone such women. Now what do *you* say?"

These teachers of the law and Pharisees had come to Jesus, not interested in justice, but eager to condemn. They saw this woman, not as a troubled sinner in need of spiritual guidance, but as a worthless reprobate deserving of death. It's true, the Old Testament law listed adultery as a capital offense, but these men with rocks in their hands were ready to set themselves up as judge, jury, and executioner without so much as an attempt to understand her life . . . or her pain. And she was *caught* in the very *act* of adultery. Ken Gire writes,

> Can you picture the scene? Peeping Pharisees nosing around her windowsill. How long did they watch? How much did they see? And were not their hearts filled with adultery when they eavesdropped on that clandestine rendezvous? . . . When they had seen enough, these guardians of morality stormed the door to the bedroom where she lay naked and defenseless. She struggled as they wrestled to subdue her. They pushed her into her clothes like a pig into a gunny sack to be taken, kicking and squealing, to market. Thus she arrives at the temple. Torn from the privacy of a stolen embrace and thrust into public shame.[1]

I don't intend to be offensive, but it cannot be very easy to catch somebody in the act of adultery unless they are extremely careless in where they choose to commit adultery—or a trap has been set to catch them. Let me ask you a question: If she was caught in the act, where is the man? Why didn't they drag him before the crowds? The Law of Moses said he was guilty and deserved to be punished as well. Maybe the man who committed the act was in on the trap. Or perhaps he was a noted man in the community—not as "expendable" as the woman. This whole scenario stinks. And do you know why? Verse 6 reveals their true motives: "They were using this question as a trap, in order to have a basis for accusing him." This woman and her sin meant nothing to these religious leaders; they couldn't care less if she were an adulteress or not. To them, she was a piece of meat, an insignificant pawn in a much larger game. This wasn't a trial, it was a trap. Warren

This woman and her sin meant nothing to these religious leaders.

Wiersbe said they were "trying to pin Jesus on the horns of a dilemma."[2] You see, if Jesus set her free, He'd be violating the Law of Moses, at least, according to the way they read the law. That would not make Him very popular with the crowds. But if He said, "Stone her"—well, that wouldn't do much for His reputation as a friend of sinners either! Still further, the Roman government didn't allow the Jews to execute anyone. That is why the Pharisees had to get the Romans to crucify Jesus for them; they weren't allowed to kill Him. If Jesus had said to stone this woman, He would have been violating Roman law and probably would have been arrested for inciting a riot. They had Jesus between a rock and a hard place—or so they thought.

So what did He do? He boldly confronted the Pharisees. Picking up at the end of verse 6:

> Jesus bent down and started to write on the ground with his finger. When they kept on questioning him, he straightened up and said to them, 'If any one of you is without sin, let him be the first to throw a stone at her.' Again he stooped down and wrote on the ground. At this, those who heard began to go away one at a time, the older ones first, until only Jesus was left, with the woman still standing there.

As they pressed in around Him to hear how He would respond, He bent down and started to write in the dust with His finger: What do you suppose He was writing? Before we attempt to answer that, I need to tell you that the Greek word used here for "write" wasn't the simple term typically used. John attached a prefix to the word that could actually render it, "To write against." Most commentators agree that Jesus was probably in some way addressing the sins of the accusers. Perhaps He was writing the Ten

> All people are guilty of something.

Commandments to remind them that all people are guilty of something. Perhaps more likely, He was writing the specific sins of some of those standing there with stones in their hands. Did He even write their names besides their sins? He certainly could have. Whatever He wrote, rather than loudly announcing their sin and inconsistency, He quietly gave them the opportunity to be convicted of their sin and to leave the scene in humility. But they didn't get the hint. They refused to back down. They kept pressing Him for a conviction. And so Jesus found that He had to be more direct. "If any one of you is without sin, let him cast the first stone." In effect He was saying, "Go ahead and throw. But before you do, make sure you've never done anything for which you're ashamed; make sure there's nothing in your past that only you and God know about—and that you want to keep that way."

There's something fair about a level playing field, isn't there? The advantage of the Pharisees was suddenly taken away, and Jesus was no longer facing only a sinful woman, but a sinful crowd. One by one, they got the hint and turned away. And do you know what Jesus did? He freely forgave this sinful woman. Verses 10-11a, "Jesus straightened up and asked her, 'Woman, where are they? Has no one condemned you?' 'No one, sir,' she said. 'Then neither do I condemn you,' Jesus declared." Without fanfare, He forgave her sin, all the while knowing He would soon have to die for her sin. Unearned, undeserved, unbelievable forgiveness! Again, Ken Gire sums it up well: "The only one qualified to condemn her, doesn't."[3]

He forgave her sin, all the while knowing He would soon have to die for her sin.

Many people are troubled by the footnote in the New International Version that says the earliest and most reliable manuscripts do not contain this portion of the Bible text. That always used to bother me. Was this just some story that was inserted later? Maybe an account that didn't really happen at all? Did some scribe make this all up and slip it in just to see if he could get away with it? What would that indicate about the authenticity of other Bible texts? William Barclay, referencing Augustine, makes a suggestion in his commentary that really intrigues me. He believes that this account was intentionally left out of many early manuscripts because people were so uncomfortable with it. It made Jesus look soft on sin. It appeared that, even without her asking for forgiveness, Jesus was willing to overlook this woman's gross immorality. It might make people think adultery was not that big a deal. And so, rather than deal with the tough questions, they just left it out altogether.[4] If that were the case, it could be argued that the story made its way back into the Bible because God intended for it to be there, and because people began to appreciate the hope this account offers to each of us. We can't earn salvation. We don't deserve to be forgiven. God freely washes us clean through the blood of Christ. But please understand, all this hinges upon Jesus' final words in verse 11, "Go now and leave your life of sin." You see, the story wasn't complete until Jesus challenged her to repent.

Forgiveness brings responsibility. That is why repentance literally means to make a U-turn. As Billy Graham explained, it's not just being sorry for sin, it's being sorry enough to quit. Jesus did not simply tell the woman she was free and clear. He directed her to straighten out those things in her life that prevented her from having a meaningful relationship with God. He challenged her to make something better of her future!

When my daughter MacKenzie was about three years old, I was tucking her into bed one night. As I leaned over her bed, she cupped my face in her hands, looked me right in the eyes, and said, "Every time I look at you, I just love you." I took out my wallet right then and said, "How much do you want?" You cannot imagine how that made me feel! That is how God feels about you! Every time He looks at you—no matter how many times you've messed up; no matter how stubborn and rebellious you've been in the past—every time He looks at you, He just loves you!

It is interesting that the word *love* is not found in John 8:1-11; however, Christ's love is revealed in nearly every verse! And it's that love which should echo through our lives as we allow God's Spirit to fill us, mold us, and use us. With that in mind, let's get really practical before we close out this chapter.

SIGNS OF LOVE

1. Love involves putting others before ourselves.

Jesus could have easily sided with the Pharisees in order to protect His reputation. The crowds may have questioned His actions, but it would have been a lot safer in the long run—no need to make the Establishment angrier than they already were. But Jesus always put others before Himself. As we think about love and sacrifice, it is tempting to have melodramatic thoughts such as, "I would lay down my life for my family if called upon to do so." That kind of macho attitude goes over big at the movies, but more often, love is putting others first in the little things.

Jesus always put others before Himself.

One summer evening, my wife Gail wasn't feeling well, so I became the designated driver for the 147 activities our kids had scheduled for that day. Before realizing what the day was going to hold, I promised my older son Aaron he could go to the movies that night with some friends. Well, things became a little more hectic that night than I had planned. I picked Aaron up at soccer practice—only they weren't finished until 6:40—and then I ran him to a friend's house to take a shower because we didn't have time to go home first. Aaron had five minutes for a shower before we needed to pick up my other son Daniel at football practice at 7:00, so we could then get Aaron back to the movie which started at 7:20. As we raced down Central Avenue toward the theater, it hit me that I owed Aaron ten dollars, but I only had three dollars in my wallet. He was counting on that money for the movies. Realizing I was cutting it close, I stopped in at the bank to get some money out of the machine. By now, it was about 7:14, and my blood pressure was starting to elevate. I ran inside, and there was a very nice old man in front of me who obviously was *not* trying to get his son to the movies in the next 4 minutes! When he was finally finished, in my hyperactive, blood-pressure-elevated condition, I punched the wrong number into the ATM—twice!—and the machine swallowed my card! For my own protection, it assured me! I jumped back in the car, breaking the news to Aaron that I didn't have the money, and I drove toward the theater, racking my brain as I went.

We counted all the change in the little holder on the dashboard. With the three bucks in my pocket, we were up to 5 dollars and *15* cents. We needed 5 dollars and *50* cents! I was 35 cents short—35 lousy cents! Now, for those of you who are health conscious, my blood pressure was now 180 over 120. Suddenly, it hit me: Carl and Karen Miller go to our church, and they own the Putt Putt Golf Course just around the next corner. I pulled into the parking lot, raced to the counter, and the nice young woman working that night cheerfully announced that neither of the Millers were there at that time. Trying to look as desperate as possible—which didn't take much by then—I explained to the nice young woman behind the counter that I was the Miller's preacher, and I *needed* 35 cents! She was probably thinking, "Boy, preachers *are* always asking for money!" Anyway, she very graciously gave me a dime and a quarter, and I got Aaron to the movies just as the last preview was winding down. Now, on the way from the Putt Putt Course to the Theater, I told Aaron, "I hope you realize how much I love you: I just begged money from a total stranger!" The things we do for love!

Romans 12:10 says, "Be devoted to one another in brotherly love. Honor one another above yourselves." Philippians 2:5 adds, "Your attitude should be the same as that of Christ Jesus." When we love somebody, we ask, "What's best for you?" "What can I do for you?" "How can I help you?" We put ourselves in their place and try to see things from their perspective. It means we listen even when we're tired or busy. We buy somebody a meal or visit them in the hospital or call just to say "Hello." We come to the defense of a coworker who is being ridiculed. We might take our wife out to dinner instead of staying home to watch a ballgame. Mother Teresa said, "Love, to be real, must cost. It must empty us of self."

"What's best for you?"
"What can I do for you?"
"How can I help you?"

2. Love demands a willingness to face tough issues.

Jesus openly confronted the sin of the Pharisees. He didn't let the adulterous woman off the hook, but commanded her to leave her life of sin. An attitude is prevalent among many today that the only loving approach to those who behave immorally is to legitimize their behavior—live and let live. "Who am I to say that someone else's behavior is improper?" If we refuse to condone what they do, we're obviously egotistical bigots with no concern for their well-being. Now granted, God didn't commission us to condemn adulterers or liars or thieves or alcoholics. But God did commission us to condemn adultery, lying, stealing, and alcohol abuse. Notice the difference—we condemn the act, not the person! Yes, God loves sinners; but He also hates sin.

There's a fascinating verse in Proverbs 27:6, "Wounds from a friend can be trusted, but an enemy multiplies kisses." Wounds from a friend *can* be trusted. Sometimes the most loving thing to do is confront someone, even though that's uncomfortable. The Bible says we're to speak the truth in love. Psychologists and social workers and pastors talk about intervention. It happens when the loved ones of an alcoholic or drug addict or some other person struggling with destructive behavior actually gather together and confront this person they love, being brutally honest about how they've been hurt and how damaging the present situation is. Sometimes the intervention works, and the pain of that confrontation actually leads to drastic change. There is also the possibility of being rebuked or ignored because the kids may rebel, your spouse may walk out, your friends may disappear, or somebody might send you a nasty letter. But to avoid confrontation for the sake of peace is not love. Romans 12:9 insists, "Love must be sincere. Hate what is evil; cling to what is good."

3. Love requires a forgiving spirit.

With no strings attached, Jesus released this woman from the guilt of her past. In effect, He wiped the slate clean and promised to never bring it up again. That is hard to do. It's human to hate; it's tough to turn the other cheek. When we have been wronged, our carnal nature wants to retaliate. Especially when an apology hasn't been offered, it's hard to let go of a wound. The most natural thing in the world is to hold a grudge. But Romans 12:21 says, "Do not be overcome by evil, but overcome evil with good." Forgiveness does not mean we forget the pain; it does not mean we automatically trust the person again; it does not mean we don't press charges if a crime has been committed. Forgiveness simply means we give up our right to get even. We refuse to let bitterness control our lives. We look at other people—even those who have hurt us deeply—and try to see them through the eyes of Christ. Our only chance to really forgive like that is to turn the hurt over to God. Ephesians 4:32 reminds us to "Be kind and compassionate to one another, forgiving each other, just as in Christ God forgave you." First Corinthians 13:5 sums it up well, "Love keeps no record of wrongs."

It's human to hate; it's tough to turn the other cheek.

4. Love persists through all circumstances.

Again, 1 Corinthians 13:7-8a says, "Love always protects, always trusts, always hopes, always perseveres. Love never fails." Several years ago, I was sitting in my office when the telephone rang. The voice on the other end of the line said, "Hi, Mark, is Steve there?" Steve was our Youth Minister. I said, "One moment, please," and put the caller on hold. I buzzed in to Steve and said, "The phone's for you. I forgot to ask who it is, but the voice sounded familiar. I'm sure it's somebody you know; I just can't place her." Steve came into my office after he finished the call and said, "Mark, that voice you didn't recognize . . . was your wife!" I knew I had been busy, but I had no idea things were that bad! Actually, we must've had a bad connection—that's my story and I'm sticking with it! Seriously, Gail is very patient with my shortcomings. One of the keys to our successful marriage is her stubborn love, in spite of me. Jesus forgave the adulterous woman in spite of her failures. He defended her in spite of her shortcomings. He loved her in spite of her sin. He is the embodiment of God's perfect, unconditional, agape love. Our job is to *echo* that kind of love.

Not only does Christlike love see us through our flaws, but it also offers itself willingly for the good of the beloved. Christ's love is, by nature, sacrificial. The Discovery Channel once aired a documentary about heroic deeds of animals. One family who lived in the country had a dog they dearly loved. He would race alongside the car every time they drove down the lane toward the highway. One particular day, he ran along beside them, barking like crazy. That just was not like him. They couldn't figure out what was wrong. Suddenly, to their horror, he raced in front of the car, and they ran over him and killed him. They were heartsick. But when they got out of the car, they heard the cries of their young son just over a little rise in the roadway. He had been riding his bike down the lane and had fallen. His foot was caught, and he couldn't get up. The couple feels certain that if the dog had not run in front of the car, they wouldn't have seen their son in time, and they would have run over him instead. They were convinced their dog had deliberately sacrificed his own life to protect their little boy. On that farm today stands a tombstone, erected as a tribute to love, both his love for them, and theirs for him. Such is the nature of love that it continues to see us through every imaginable circumstance.

NOTES

[1]Ken Gire, *Moments with the Savior* (Grand Rapids: Zondervan, 1998), p. 193.

[2]Warren Wiersbe, *Be Alive* (Wheaton, IL: Victor Books, a division of SP Publications, 1986), p. 96.

[3]Gire, *Moments*, p. 195.

[4]William Barclay, *The Gospel of John*, vol. 2, rev. ed. (Philadelphia: Westminster, 1975), pp. 290-292.

Reflecting on Lesson One

1. Can you remember a time when someone demonstrated Christlike love to you? How did it make you feel?

2. Have you ever been forced to confront someone, only to have your intentions misunderstood? What happened? How could you have handled things differently?

3. What is one way you could demonstrate love to a friend or family member this week?

Consider this:

Look again at the life situations mentioned at the end of the Study Introduction—a gambling spouse, a teenager using drugs, a child in a temper. Do you feel happy under such conditions? Could you feel joy in spite of these or similar painful circumstances? James 1:2-4 says we should consider facing trials a joy. How would you describe the difference between happiness and joy?

2

ECHOING GOD'S JOY

In this lesson:

- The definition of joy
- Barriers to joy
- The Source of joy
- The formula for joy

My family and I vacationed for several days one summer around Ashville, North Carolina. I love waterfalls, so I dragged the kids to several while we were there. One of the falls stands out in my mind, not because it was the biggest or the prettiest, but because it was the most fun. I decided I didn't want to swim, and my older son Aaron wasn't feeling well, but I grabbed my camera and set out with the rest of the family toward a waterfall where they planned to get in the river and splash around for a while. We never dreamed this would be a highlight of the whole vacation. After walking nearly two miles, we came to these falls that must have been twenty feet high. The water fell over ten feet of very slick rock, and then dropped another ten feet into a large pool at the bottom.

Several teenagers were there wading out into the river, sliding down over the falls, and landing in the pool. They would then pull themselves back up the steep slope by hanging onto a huge rope that had been tied to a tree at the far side of the falls. My kids, Daniel and MacKenzie, took one look and couldn't wait to try it. Gail took one look . . . and *agreed* to try it. I just couldn't wait to get the pictures! I shot an entire roll of film as they each came flying over the falls and splashed down in the pool below. It was incredible to watch! The look on their faces was hilarious! Isn't it fun to watch people who are having a great time? Especially children! When they throw themselves into some activity and they laugh uncontrollably while doing it, we get glimpses of unrestrained exhilaration. That's what memories are made of.

Isn't it fun to watch people who are having a great time?

The Bible says God wants His children to experience joy. Not necessarily a "flying over the waterfall" kind of exhilaration, but a deep and abiding sense of well-being. "The fruit of the Spirit is love, joy, peace, patience, kindness, goodness, faithfulness, gentleness and self-control. Against such things there is no law" (Galatians 5:22-23). Read that list again more carefully. The fruit of the Spirit is joy.

And yet, do you ever find yourself wondering, "If I'm a Christian, and the fruit of God's Spirit living inside of me is joy, why don't I *feel* joyful? Why is life so hard? Why does my attitude hit rock bottom so often? What is joy all about anyway, and where can I get some?" Perhaps God's Word can offer some answers. James 1:2-4 suggest, "Consider it pure joy, my brothers, whenever you face trials of many kinds, because you know that the testing of your faith develops perseverance. Perseverance must finish its work so that you may be mature and complete, not lacking anything." Paul adds in 2 Corinthians 7:4b, "In all our troubles, my joy knows no bounds." Frankly, both of those statements are fairly startling. James says we should actually rejoice when we are going through trials because it is the trials that make us strong. Paul says that despite his numerous problems—not little problems like homework or traffic or computer failure, but big problems like deprivation and persecution and prison—in spite of those problems, his joy is beyond measure. I don't know about you, but those statements suggest to me that God's definition of joy must be far different from the world's definition.

THE DEFINITION OF JOY

The world typically equates joy with happiness; however, there is a critical distinction between the two. Happiness is based upon circumstances. Have you ever said something like, "If I only had ____, then I would be happy"? What was in the *blank*? A new car? A bigger house? A dream vacation? A husband? A *different* husband? What would it take to make you happy? I recently looked at a brand new Nikon D100 digital camera. Photography is a passion of mine, and I had been reading for weeks about this latest model to hit the market. I finally got to see one up close. It is an amazing camera! Granted, it costs $2000, so I'm not holding my breath, but it is incredible! I figure a camera like that would make me happy—for about three days! Don't get me wrong: I would use it and enjoy it for a lot longer than that. But a camera isn't going to keep me happy no matter how many bells and whistles it has on it. There is no *thing* in this world that can make anyone truly happy.

Happiness is based on outward circumstances.

You see, happiness is based on outward circumstances—the physical comforts and pleasures and cameras of life. And those things, by nature, are temporary. They come and go, oftentimes very quickly. I talked to my friend Jim not long ago. Jim and his wife Eleanora were driving through Tennessee on vacation when their SUV suddenly hydroplaned on the wet pavement. They went off the road and rolled over four times. It's a miracle they weren't killed. I will admit, they have much to be thankful for. But you know what else? They never intended to spend their vacation lying around the house, nursing cuts and bruises, a concussion and sore muscles. One minute, life was cruising along pretty well; the next minute, everything in their lives was turned upside down—literally.

It's a simple reality: Happiness depends on pleasurable circumstances, and God never promised that we would always be happy. In fact, the words "happy" and "happiness" appear only 27 times in the entire New International Version of the Bible. On the other hand, the words "joy" and "rejoice" are found 320 times! Joy may be a distant cousin of happiness, but they are not the same thing.

While happiness is based on circumstances, joy is based upon a relationship with Jesus Christ. When we have a dynamic relationship with the Lord, our joy prevails regardless of our circumstances. First Peter 1:8-9 says this concerning Jesus: "Though you have not seen him, you love him; and even though you do not see him now, you believe in him and are filled with an inexpressible and glorious joy, for you are receiving the goal of your faith, the salvation of your souls." Even though we can't see Him, we know He is there. We love Him because He loves us, gave His life for us, and promises to bring us to heaven. And because we have that kind of relationship with Him, we are *filled* with joy. The reality of Christ's presence and the incredible hope of eternity enable us not only to endure, but to prevail.

The reality of Christ's presence and the incredible hope of eternity enable us not only to endure, but to prevail.

How does that woman in the cancer ward maintain such a bright and optimistic outlook? It is not her physical condition; it is her relationship with Christ. How can that inmate on death row exude such a positive attitude? It is not his living arrangements; it is his newfound relationship with Christ. How did that victim of childhood sexual abuse leave the scars behind and discover once again the will to live and the ability to love? It all hinges on a relationship with Jesus Christ. Unfortunately, many of us still struggle with joy even though we are in far better circumstances than those. Several barriers often keep joy just out of reach.

THE BARRIERS TO JOY

1. Negative Upbringing

Ephesians 6:4 insists, "Fathers, do not exasperate your children; instead, bring them up in the training and instruction of the Lord." Unfortunately, many fathers—and mothers—are exasperating. You may have grown up in a negative home. Maybe your parents constantly criticized you; there was little laughter there. Maybe you even lived in fear. When I was growing up, I lived in a home full of joy. We laughed together, and we played together. My brother and sister and I have always been the best of friends. But one summer when I was about twelve years old, I spent a week with a friend, and his family argued and complained and criticized each other all the time. The day I came home, I ended up in a big argument with my sister. In the middle of the quarrel, I called a time-out, and said, "Vicki, I'm sorry. I've been around fighting all week, and I think it just rubbed off." One week, and it affected me! If you spent your entire childhood in an environment of criticism, abuse, complaining, and profanity, joy may be a real challenge for you. I once heard a Christian psychologist share about a patient of his who grew up in a home without joy. When he was a little boy, he would slip next door and sit on his neighbor's front porch at suppertime and just listen through the screen door as that family shared a meal together. He longed for what they had, but he never got it.

Just because joy is a challenge for you, don't think it is an impossibility. Remember joy comes as a result of the Spirit-led life.

2. Unresolved Guilt

Another barrier to joy is unresolved guilt. Often the guilt is unfounded: something happened in the past that you have already repented of, and you know in your mind that you have been forgiven by God, but you just can't seem to let go of the guilt. Maybe you are divorced, and you know deep down it was your fault. Or you got in trouble with law, and the crime is on your permanent record, and it keeps coming up on job applications. Maybe there was a moral failure, and you have left a string of broken promises in your wake, and if you ever wrote your life story, the title would be *If Only*. If that is you, let me remind you of this reality: If you have confessed that sin before God, and you have truly repented of it—you have stopped doing it—then the guilt is from Satan; it is not from God. God promises to cast our sin into the depths of the sea and forget it.

Second Corinthians 7:10 states that "Godly sorrow brings repentance that leads to salvation and leaves no regret, but worldly sorrow brings death." Your sorrow may very well be worldly sorrow which brings death. On the other hand, the guilt you are feeling may be entirely justified. There is secret sin in your life right now—perhaps it is even written in your calendar—you know it is coming this Tuesday after work while your wife is out of town. Understand, we will never have joy in our lives while we are harboring secret sin. King Arthur, in the musical production of *Camelot*, said, "One cannot be wicked and happy at the same time." The Bible admits that sin brings pleasure for a season; but true joy cannot coexist with a guilty conscience.

Godly sorrow leaves no regret.

3. Unrealistic Expectations

Another barrier to joy is unrealistic expectations. If you are a perfectionist like I tend to be, you know we often set ourselves up to be let down. We have such high hopes of how the day is going to unfold that no 24-hour period of time could possibly live up to the anticipation. Rather than allowing for a few setbacks along the way, we are blindsided by them, and then we are crushed when our plans have to change. Or we put incredible expectations on our spouse, our friends, or our coworkers, and when they don't live up to those expectations, we become disillusioned. We head off on vacation expecting fair weather, few mosquitoes, family camaraderie, and no sunburns. And then somebody is not speaking to somebody else before we are out of the neighborhood, and it rains for six days straight, and what do we do? We sacrifice joy on the altar of perfection. Instead, we should let life unfold in a realistic manner. We learn to accept the inevitable. We choose to see interruptions as opportunities. The apostle Paul wrote in Philippians 4:11b, "I have learned to be content whatever the circumstances." That's a worthwhile goal.

Let life unfold in a realistic manner.

4. Wounded Ego

Still further, a wounded ego can rob us of joy. Perhaps someone has criticized you, or embarrassed you, or hurt your feelings. Maybe your girlfriend is ignoring you or your husband has ridiculed you in public, and you feel unloved and unwanted. When I was in high school, the preachers in Louisville played an annual basketball game against some of the high school students from the area churches. Several of the ministers had played ball in college, and they were still good athletes. As a matter of fact, they were killing us. Well, to add insult to injury, at one point during the fourth quarter, one of them put his jersey on his little boy who was about six years old and checked him into the game in place of the man I was supposed to be guarding. Of course I wasn't going to guard him, but when they passed him the ball, he hit a 15-foot jump shot right in my face. The crowd went wild. The next time down the court, they passed him the ball again, and I just held my hand up. Honest! I didn't jump at all! Well, I blocked his shot, and the entire crowd booed me. Vehemently! I think my mom even said to the woman next to her, "Who is that mean red-headed boy?" I wanted to crawl in a hole! It's hard to have joy when you hate yourself.

5. Unpleasant Circumstances

This is likely the most common barrier to joy. It is easy to be positive and pleasant when things are great with your family, your job, your health, your church, your finances. But what happens when your teenager rebels, or you lose your job, or your health breaks, or your small group becomes divisive, or your finances crumble? What happens to your outlook when your circumstances turn sour? One of my favorite passages of Scripture in the Old Testament is found in Habakkuk 3:17-19. I want you to remember this because someday you are going to meet Habakkuk in heaven, and he is going to ask you, "What did you think of my book?" and you would be embarrassed, if it weren't for what I'm about to tell you! Consider what he wrote:

It is easy to be positive and pleasant when things are great.

> Though the fig tree does not bud and there are no grapes on the vines, though the olive crop fails and the fields produce no food, though there are no sheep in the pen and no cattle in the stalls, yet I will rejoice in the Lord, I will be joyful in God my Savior. The Sovereign Lord is my strength; he makes my feet like the feet of a deer, he enables me to go on the heights."

Did you catch that? "Even if everything goes wrong in my life—if all of my external circumstances absolutely stink—*yet* will I rejoice in the Lord!" Why? He explains in the last verse, "The Sovereign Lord is my strength." He is our source of joy.

THE SOURCE OF JOY

Did you realize that we serve a joyful God? That may not come as a surprise to you, but I confess, that thought was revolutionary for me. When I think of God, I tend to focus on His holiness, His power, His wisdom, and His majesty. I think of His mercy, compassion, tenderness, and love. I even realize that He promises to give joy to us. But I don't often picture God being joyful. Yet the premise of this book remains: each unique fruit of the Spirit begins with God and then echoes through our lives. We don't simply receive these character traits as a gift; they emanate from heaven, and then reverberate through our lives. Joseph Marmion said, *"Joy is the echo of God's life within us."*

Nehemiah 8:10b states, "Do not grieve, for the joy of the Lord is your strength." It is God's joy that strengthens us. The prophet Isaiah promised in Isaiah 62:5b: "As a bridegroom rejoices over his bride, so will your God rejoice over you." One cannot get much more intimate, more personal, more passionate than a groom rejoicing over his bride, but that is the picture Isaiah uses for God's joy over us, His children. And then there is Zephaniah 3:17, another of my very favorite Old Testament verses that should help shape our entire view of God: "The Lord your God is with you, he is mighty to save. He will take great delight in you, he will quiet you with his love, he will rejoice over you with singing." I want you to think about that: The God of heaven rejoices over you with singing! I wonder what it would be like to hear God sing. I imagine sometimes it is loud and strong, like rolling thunder; at other times, it is as gentle as a breeze rustling the treetops on a summer day. He sings over us, because we bring Him joy. And in the process, He grants joy to us as well!

> The God of heaven rejoices over you with singing!

Jesus modeled a joyful life. It was one of His dominant personality traits. You won't see that in most of the movies which portray Jesus. He usually looks serious, even somber. You wonder how somebody so bland could have had such an impact on the world. But Jesus was not that way at all! Oh, He was certainly serious at times, and He was never flippant about important things. But He knew what it was like to have a good time, and He always exuded joy. It was the stodgy old Pharisees who accused Him of being a glutton and a drunkard. Why? Because He went to parties; He celebrated life; His contagious personality attracted others. His first miracle came at a wedding feast—a party. And in sermons, He told jokes. We may not think of it that way, but in ancient Jewish culture, exaggeration was a pivotal form of humor. He talked about a camel going through the eye of a needle, a man with a log in his eye trying to help another man get a speck out of his eye, a servant who owed his master billions of dollars, and the Pharisees themselves who were nitpicky about little things and so oblivious to the big things. He said they would strain a gnat out of their soup but then turn right around and swallow a camel! Jesus was a funny guy! One of the things I really like about the Easter Pageant at Southeast Christian Church in Louisville, Kentucky, is that Jesus laughs with His friends, He plays with the children, and He does a Jewish dance with His disciples. That is the real Jesus—He radiated joy!

Think about the night before His death, when He was literally carrying the weight of the world on His shoulders. His enemies were closing in; Judas had already sold Him out; when He came into the Last Supper, His disciples were arguing over which of them was the greatest; and He was about to be condemned and murdered for the sins of the whole world. Even then, Jesus talked about joy. In John 15:9-11 Jesus says,

> As the Father has loved me, so have I loved you. Now remain in my love. If you obey my commands, you will remain in my love, just as I have obeyed my Father's commands and remain in his love. I have told you this so that my joy may be in you and that your joy may be complete.

Notice, He did not just promise to give them joy. He said, "My joy will be in you." Hebrews 12:2 says, "Let us fix our eyes on Jesus, the author and perfecter of our faith, who for the joy set before him endured the cross, scorning its shame, and sat down at the right hand of the throne of God." Jesus did not enjoy the cross—far from it. He said in the Garden of Gethsemane before He was arrested that His soul was overwhelmed with sorrow to the point of death. He was not a masochist, a glutton for punishment who delighted in horrific torture. He dreaded the crucifixion more than we can possibly imagine. But He endured it for the joy that was to come—for the joy He would bring to us!

Jesus endured the cross for the joy He would bring to us!

Not only do we see joy as a trait of God the Father and God the Son. The Holy Spirit transfers that joy to us. The fruit of the Spirit—the product of God's Spirit within us—is joy. The Apostle Paul commended the church of Thessalonica in 1 Thessalonians 1:6, "In spite of severe suffering, you welcomed the message with the joy given by the Holy Spirit." Where did the joy come from? The Spirit of God.

If you are struggling with joy today, my very first question to you is, "Have you surrendered your life to Jesus Christ?" Not, "Are you a member of the church?" Not, "Have you ever been baptized?" Not, "Do you come to church every Sunday, and pray before every meal, and give a tenth of your income to the Lord?"

All those things are important, but they will not bring you joy. Joy comes when you make Jesus Christ the Lord of your life. God created joy, Jesus modeled it, and the Holy Spirit transfers it to us. But we will never have it—we will never echo it—until Jesus is Lord. That brings us to this final summary.

THE FORMULA FOR JOY

It is such a stereotypical "Sunday School" formula that I hesitate to even mention it. It sounds trite really, like something you would teach to little children. But the truth is, a life of joy absolutely *requires* the appropriate priorities in life. And so I will remind you of an acrostic that has been repeated so often because it is absolutely true.

JESUS

Jesus must be first in your life: That's the Letter "J" of JOY. Jesus. Jesus said in John 15:5, "I am the vine; you are the branches. If a man remains in me and I in him, he will bear much fruit; apart from me you can do nothing." If He is not first, you'll never have joy. Never.

C.S. Lewis, a brilliant scholar and college professor, was also a devout atheist. Following a skeptical but intensive study of the Bible, he became a Christian. In fact, he once confessed, *"I came kicking and screaming into the Kingdom of God."* He did not want to believe, but he found he could not deny the truth any longer. Following his conversion, he wrote a book entitled, *Surprised by Joy*. He said the new sense of well-being and contentment was something he never anticipated; however, once Jesus became his priority, he realized the essence of true life.

Remember that scene in the movie *Chariots of Fire* when Eric Liddell talks to his sister Jenny about his running? Eric was a dedicated Christian on his way to the mission field in China, but also an Olympic sprinter. When he put China on hold for a few months until the Olympics were over, Jenny didn't understand the rationale of that decision. Eric took her up into the hills of Scotland, their homeland, and said this: "God made me for a purpose, Jenny—for China. But He also made me fast, and when I run, I feel His pleasure." Joy comes when we use our gifts and abilities, our time and our treasure, to please the Lord.

Others

The "O" stands for others. Paul wrote in 2 Timothy 1:3-4, "I thank God . . . as night and day I constantly remember you in my prayers. Recalling your tears, I long to see you, so that I may be filled with joy." Paul wanted to see Timothy so that he could encourage and strengthen his son in the faith, all the while knowing that as he ministered to Timothy, it would renew his own sense of joy.

Millard Fuller, founder of Habitat for Humanity, was a millionaire by age 29. A very successful businessman, he paid a high price for the American dream, sacrificing his health, his integrity, and his family on the altar of success. When his wife Linda, lonely and unhappy, went away to stay with a pastor friend and his family for a few weeks, Millard realized that his life was drastically out of balance. He went to Linda, and the two of them admitted that all they were living for was superficial; their lives were empty and their marriage was in shambles. However, rather than throwing in the towel, the Fullers chose to redirect the entire course of their lives. That very night, they decided to sell everything and dedicate themselves to helping the poor. Linda said they were not simply giving up money and the things money could buy; they were giving up a whole way of life that was killing them. They have since devoted their lives to building homes for underprivileged families all over the world.

If you find your joy slipping, maybe you need to invest yourself in someone else who is hurting. It doesn't require a career change or starting an international ministry; it is a simple matter of shifting your priorities toward others. Take the time to listen to a friend who is hurting; send a note of encouragement to a college student during finals week; do some house repairs for a widow at church; mow your neighbor's grass; mow your preacher's grass! Jesus pointed out that even a cup of cold water shared in His name speaks volumes about the condition of a person's heart.

If you find your joy slipping, maybe you need to invest yourself in someone else who is hurting.

Yourself

Finally, the letter "Y" stands for yourself. As Christians, we don't ignore our own needs to the point of deprivation and self-loathing. Jesus gave us the Golden Rule, "Love your neighbor *as* you love yourself." We put Christ first and others before ourselves. Then, when we do take care of ourselves and meet our own needs, we are doing it for the specific purpose of serving the Lord and serving others more effectively. Joy does not mean we ignore ourselves; it means we look upward and outward before we look inward.

Furthermore, Jesus assured His disciples in John 16:22, "Now is your time of grief, but I will see you again and you will rejoice, and no one will take away your joy." As we remember our destiny—that place of eternal joy—it reminds us that we can also rejoice in the here-and-now, because our sins are forgiven and our hope is secure.

Dr. Leroy Lawson, in his book, *God's Way to a More Perfect You,* wrote about a Mrs. Miller who had a mastectomy due to cancer. Mrs. Miller was a vibrant Christian woman, and as she lay on a gurney in the hospital hallway, she heard the woman next to her sobbing. Concerned, she asked the woman "What's wrong?"

The woman spat back, "What do you mean, what's wrong? Look where I am. I've got cancer."

"So do I."

"Yes, but I had surgery for the removal of a breast, and now I've got lumps on the other side."

"So have I."

"But that's not all. These treatments make me violently ill."

"I know. Me too."

"Besides all that, I'm in my 50s and I think I'm going to die."

"I think I'm going to die too."

"Well, how can you lie there so [expletive] peaceful?"

"Have you tried praying?"

"Of course I've prayed. I've gone to every church in the area. I've prayed everything from Christian Scientist to Buddhist to Baptist, and you know what? None of them worked."

"I know why."

"You do? Why?"

"You . . . think your essential problem is to get rid of cancer, but what you really need is Jesus." After some further discussion and a lot of tears, the woman asked Mrs. Miller to pray with her, and the nurses later reported a dynamic change in the woman's attitude. She was literally never the same person from that moment.

She began to learn a truth that day which we all must discover for ourselves: Joy is never found in perfect health or happy circumstances or an easy life. True joy can only be found in a relationship with Jesus Christ. As we grow in that relationship, we will echo His joy more fully.[1]

Joy is never found in perfect health or happy circumstances or an easy life; only in a relationship with Christ.

NOTES

[1]Leroy Lawson, *God's Way to a More Perfect You* (Joplin, MO: College Press, 1993), pp. 42-44.

Reflecting on Lesson Two

1. How would you distinguish between joy and happiness? Can you think of a time when you were able to maintain joy despite your circumstances?

2. What are the pivotal barriers to joy in your life? How do you deal with them?

3. Which of the three priorities—Jesus, Others, Yourself—is hardest for you to keep in its proper perspective? What is one thing you can do this week to help bring it into balance?

Consider this:

In Matthew 8 we find the story of Jesus calming the storm. When they turned to Jesus, the disciples experienced peace immediately. How often has that happened to you? Sometimes we wish God were a magician at our call to calm all the storms of life and make everything better; however, that is seldom our experience. Tell of a time when you were in the midst of a storm and Jesus brought peace to your heart while the storm continued to rage.

3

ECHOING GOD'S PEACE

In this lesson:

- Storms come to everyone
- Storms produce fear
- The difference between fear and worry
- The comfort of God

I love the story about the man who was jogging through a cemetery late one night when he stumbled in the darkness and fell into a newly dug grave. He slowly got to his feet and evaluated the situation. Scratching and clawing for all he was worth, he tried everything in his power to climb out, but he just couldn't do it. He finally resigned himself to the fact that he would have to wait for somebody to come along in the morning and give him a hand. Not long afterward, another jogger came through the cemetery and fell into the same grave. He also tried to climb the steep walls, but with no success. All of a sudden, he felt a hand on his shoulder. A voice said, "It's no use. You can't get out." BUT HE DID!

Have you ever fallen into a hole so deep you thought there was no way out? Have you ever been hit by a crisis so overwhelming that you thought there was no means of escape? Ever had the props suddenly knocked out from under you? Ever been abruptly and unexpectedly bowled over by a disaster or emergency? We all face unexpected storms at some point in our lives. And yet hardships don't have to be unforeseen to be overwhelming. Some trials are expected but still brutal. For the college student, it is finals week; for the CPA, it is April 15th; for the allergy sufferer, there is ragweed season. On a deeper level, for the family member of a terminally ill patient, it might be a long-expected death. There are those moments in life that are anticipated, but still difficult, even heartbreaking.

Have you ever been hit by a crisis so overwhelming that you thought there was no means of escape?

Furthermore, there are the daily frustrations of life. From traffic jams to the stomach flu, from an irritable boss to a strong-willed preschooler, people and circumstances can rob us of peace. How do you react when life throws you a curve? What's your attitude when life tumbles in? Galatians 5:22-23 says, "The fruit of the Spirit is love, joy, peace, patience, kindness, goodness, faithfulness, gentleness, and self-control. Against such things there is no law." The fruit of the Spirit is peace, and yet the storms of life often render peace an elusive quality.

It certainly was for the Disciples of Jesus. In Matthew chapter 8, they discovered just how quickly peace can disappear. They were out in a boat on the Sea of Galilee when a storm of such magnitude came up that they feared for their very lives. Their experience proves once again that Jesus offers the only hope for true peace. But remember, it is a *fruit* of the Spirit—it is a *product* of God's presence—and it is only possible through the power of Jesus Christ. Now, the story begins with an unexpected storm.

AN UNEXPECTED STORM

The evening began calmly enough. After teaching the multitudes all day, Jesus suggested to the disciples a trip across the lake for some peace and quiet. However, instead of peace and quiet, their journey suddenly went from calm to chaos. Matthew 8:23-24 depicts, "Then Jesus got into the boat and his disciples followed him. Without warning, a furious storm came up on the lake, so that the waves swept over the boat. But Jesus was sleeping." The Sea of Galilee is notorious for ferocious, unpredictable storms. Located 600 feet below sea level, the cool air from the mountains around it often comes blasting down across the water. William Barclay comments: *"The storms on the Sea of Galilee combine suddenness and violence in a unique way."*[1] The disciples couldn't very well listen to the Weather Channel before setting out, so they struck out from shore, unaware of the impending danger until it had them completely surrounded.

The hard reality is that life can turn upside down suddenly and unexpectedly. Have you seen that Internet photograph making the rounds which shows a Great White shark leaping out of the water to attack a sailor who is dangling from the ladder of a hovering helicopter? Fortunately for that sailor, the picture is a fake. According to National Geographic's Web Site, it is actually two photographs spliced together, a U.S. Air Force photo taken near the Golden Gate Bridge during training exercises, and another of a shark from the South African coast. Despite the origin of the picture, whoever doctored those images created a hair-raising summary of how a lot of us feel at times—like we're hanging on for dear life, and a man-eating monster is lunging in our direction.

There is something very important you need to notice from this text. Even though the disciples were with Jesus in the boat, doing exactly what He told them to do, they were still overcome by a life-threatening storm. Sometimes people believe that if they walk with God, life will always be smooth sailing. If they can just manage to have enough faith, they will never get sick, never lose their job, always face pleasant circumstances. That kind of theology is a slap in the face to the life of our Savior. God had one Son without sin, but no Son without sorrow. Jesus knows what it feels like to be ignored, hated, misquoted, abused, and put to death.

God had one Son without sin, but no Son without sorrow.

Do you remember Jesus' parable of the wise and foolish builders? One man built on a rock foundation, the other built on sand; not long afterward, the rainy season began. When the rain fell, it fell on both houses; when the storm raged, it beat against both houses; when the floodwater rose, it threatened both houses. The man who built wisely was not exempt from the storm, but his house stood because of the sure foundation. Just because we're Christians, we're not exempt from car wrecks or malignancies, tornadoes or termites. Jesus Christ doesn't promise exemption, but a sure foundation.

It's been 14 or 15 years now, but I'll never forget the Sunday afternoon that my friend Charles called the house to tell me his brother Kelly had just been killed in a car accident. Kelly and his fiancee had a fight, he stormed out of the house, sped off in his truck, and hadn't been gone five minutes when he flipped over going around a curve and was killed instantly. Walking into that hospital, Charles and I were instantly confronted with Kelly's 25-year-old broken body lying on a cold, stainless steel table. When Charles crumbled to the ground in overwhelming grief, it was almost more than I could bear. Maybe you've been there, and you understand that pain all too well; you've experienced a similar devastating loss. Or your teenager has suddenly announced, "I have a drinking problem." Or your boss walked into your office and said, "We're going to have to cut back, and you have the least seniority. I'm sorry." We have all been there, because suffering is unavoidable.

Maybe you have heard the quote: "A ship is safe in the harbor, but that's not what ships are made for." Well, the fact is, ships might be *safer* in the harbor, but they are not always safe, even there; and I can say two words which will prove that: Pearl Harbor. Unexpected storms come into every life.

Ships might be *safer* in the harbor, but they are not always safe, even there.

AN UNDERSTANDABLE FEAR

One Peanuts comic strip showed Charlie Brown and Peppermint Patty leaning up against a tree talking. Peppermint Patty asks, "What do you think security is, Chuck?"

"Security? Security is sleeping in the back seat of the car. When you're a little kid, and you've been somewhere with your mom and dad, and it's night, and you're riding home in the car, you can sleep in the back seat. You don't have to worry about anything. Your mom and dad are in the front seat, and they do all the worrying. They take care of everything."

Peppermint Patty smiles and says, "That's real neat!"

Suddenly Charlie Brown's tone changes: "But it doesn't last! Suddenly, you're grown up, and . . . it's over, you'll never get to sleep in the back seat again!"

"Never?"

"Absolutely never!" The last frame shows Peppermint Patty with a stricken look on her face, grabbing for Charlie Brown: "Hold my hand, Chuck!"

Sometimes life is not very secure; sometimes fear is understandable. That night on the Sea of Galilee, the disciples found themselves in grave danger. The end of verse 24 explains, "Jesus was sleeping. The disciples went and woke him, saying, "Lord, save us! We're going to drown!" Jesus' twelve companions did everything humanly possible to keep the boat afloat and save their lives: They rowed, they bailed, they lowered the sails—but it was no use. Think how violent this storm must have been for these seasoned fishermen to fear for their lives! All of a sudden it dawned on them that Jesus wasn't helping at all. He wasn't rowing, He wasn't bailing—He was sleeping! Jesus lived His life in such peace, such rhythm—with such faith—that when chaos came, He was prepared to face it calmly.

Sometimes fear is understandable.

Well, the disciples immediately woke Him up. In fact, Mark tells us in his Gospel that they demanded: "Don't you care that we're about to drown?" Have you ever felt that way? "God, my life's a mess down here. Don't you care?" "My family's falling apart, I'm lonely and depressed, and I'm losing my mind. Does that mean anything to you?" God understands those feelings. It is not wrong to cry out to Him during times of fear and stress. Who better to cry out to? But there is more to Christianity than having God as a life preserver. You see, a lot of people think surrendering to Christ in the first place is like buying life insurance: They know they need it, but they buy it hoping they will never have to use it. And so, they go through life figuring they won't bother God if He doesn't bother them. Then all hell breaks loose, and they wonder where God is.

Understand, Jesus was not asleep in the boat that night because of a lack of concern. He was asleep because He had not been summoned yet! The disciples pulled the old, "When all else fails, pray" routine. They fought with all their might first, then they turned to Jesus. Prayer should not be a desperate S.O.S. call, it should be a consistent priority. We need close contact with Jesus no matter what kind of circumstances we are facing. Instead of waiting until the storm is raging full blast, we ought to be spending time with the Lord, rain or shine.

Jesus was asleep because He had not been summoned yet!

One good reason is because sometimes life is scary. My parents' friend, Cecil Byrd, a missionary in Mozambique, was murdered by a gang of armed men who burst into the compound where he and his family lived. The abduction of Elizabeth Smart, and stories like it, haunt most parents. As I reread accounts of the horrific events of September 11, 2001, the fear and anxiety of watching those disasters unfold come flooding back. Sometimes life is scary, and to casually act like serious threats are no big deal is both unwise and unrealistic. Fear in this world is understandable. The only cure for fear is trusting God.

AN UNBELIEVABLE RESCUE

How did the Lord resolve the fears of His disciples? He dramatically calmed their storm. Matthew 8:26, "He replied, 'You of little faith, why are you so afraid?' Then he got up and rebuked the winds and the waves, and it was completely calm." Jesus rebuked the storm, and it worked! Suddenly, everything became completely calm. In the blink of an eye, twenty-foot breakers gave way to a sea of glass. One moment, they could hardly hear the cry of their own voices; the next moment, they could hear a pin drop. They moved instantly from total panic to perfect peace. The wind stopped blowing, the waves stopped breaking over the boat. Everything was completely calm. Ken Gire writes, "The disciples have seen Jesus give strength to lame legs, sight to blind eyes, and health to a centurion's servant. But they have never seen him do anything like this. It is the greatest unleashing of raw power they have ever witnessed."[2]

What kind of impact did it have? Verse 27 concludes, "The men were amazed and asked, 'What kind of man is this? Even the winds and the waves obey him!'" Again, Mark tells us in his account of this event that the disciples were terrified by what Jesus had done. It is interesting, their fear of the storm gave way to an even greater fear: This was no mere man they were following; he was not just a prophet. As Ken Gire concluded, Jesus had just done "what only God himself could do."[3] The disciples were overwhelmed with the realization that Jesus was the Son of God.

Where do you go when you're afraid? The disciples learned a valuable lesson that night on the Sea of Galilee. Because Jesus is the eternal Son of God, He can be trusted to calm our fears. Even if the storm had raged on, even if the boat had sunk, trusting Jesus was their only hope. He is the only source of peace.

A fascinating verse can be found in the Old Testament book of Nahum, chapter one, verse 3. "The Lord is slow to anger and great in power. . . . His way is in the whirlwind and the storm." That seems very appropriate for this text: The Lord is actually in the storm. However, it is the last part of that verse which really grabbed me. In the New Living Translation, it says, "The billowing clouds are the dust of his feet." Those thunderheads that look so threatening? Why, that's just God walking around up there looking down on us to make sure everything is okay. Granted, that concept is more poetic than scientific, but it is a great perspective. God is watching over us, and ultimately, everything will be all right.

Those thunderheads that look so threatening? Why, that's just God walking around.

Listen to Christ's words in John 14:27, "Peace I leave with you; my peace I give you. I do not give to you as the world gives. Do not let your hearts be troubled and do not be afraid." How does the world give peace? We get all kinds of advice: "Take this pill and relax"; "drink this cocktail and forget"; "buy this new mattress and sleep better than ever"; "buy this exercise machine and feel better than ever"; "go on this cruise and live better than ever." Jesus doesn't offer superficial, temporary peace. It's not Band-Aid relief; He offers the real deal. He is the Prince of Peace, and He wants to calm the storms of your life.

Early in her career, Christian recording artist Amy Grant experienced a time of personal crisis. She appeared to have it all together, but the personal and career pressures had become so great, she decided to flee to Europe leaving her troubles behind. *Aspire* magazine later interviewed Grant, and she explained that her older sister came to the rescue. She convinced her to stay and work things out.

> She just marched right up to me and said, "Fine. Go to Europe. Leave it all behind. Start your life again. But before you go, you have to do one thing. You have to go to my little girl, and tell her how you can sing that Jesus can help her though anything in her life, but that He couldn't help you."[4]

I want to offer several lessons as we close out this chapter to help you understand how Jesus calms storms today—to help you understand how peace can be a product of God's Holy Spirit inside of us.

1. Worry is a sin, but fear is not.

Fear is a normal response that nearly everyone experiences when facing threatening situations. King David wrote in Psalm 56:3, "When I am afraid, I will trust in you." Notice, he did not say *if* I become afraid, but *when.* Fear comes when danger is near, and that is totally understandable. However, worry comes when we conjure up the threatening situations in our own mind; when we stew and fret about all the potential dangers that *could* happen, but probably will not. Jesus commands us not to worry because worry takes our focus off of God's plan for our lives; it causes us to doubt the care of God. Trust and worry cannot coexist.

> Fear can serve as a trigger to remind us to trust.

So what do we do with our fear? It can serve as a trigger to remind us to trust. It is like a warning light on the dashboard of the car that says it is time to buy gas or change the oil or check the engine. We can ignore the light and face the consequences, or we can heed its warning and travel more safely. When we become afraid, we can live in a constant state of panic, or we can allow the fear to remind us to turn to God. Do you remember the September 11th cellular phone call from Todd Beamer aboard United Airlines Flight 93 to Lisa Jefferson, the Airfone Operator? As he described conditions on the plane, at one point he cried out, *"Oh Jesus, please help us."* Then, as the two of them recited the *Lord's Prayer* together over the phone, Lisa said she could hear screams in the background: Passengers were crying out, *"God help us; Jesus help us."* And He did. He gave them the courage and strength to stand up to their enemies. You see, when we're afraid, the fear itself reminds us to turn to God for strength.

2. God does not always prevent trouble from coming.

This may not be a very comforting thought, but it is the truth. And I would rather tell you a hard truth than give you a false promise. Jesus said in John 16:33, "In me you may have peace. In this world you will have trouble. But take heart! I have overcome the world." Jesus makes a very important promise in that verse, and it is not what you might expect. He *promised* that we would have *trouble*! "In this world, you *will* have trouble." Now, He also assured us we have the opportunity for peace: "In me, you *may* have peace." Notice the difference: "You *will* have trouble." "You *may* have peace." At some point, each one of us will face a storm that can only be handled with God's help. We must decide if the world's trouble or God's peace will win. If you are not facing that pressure right now, don't feel left out. Your time will come! It is true. You shouldn't go looking for trouble, but you should not be shocked by it either. When it comes, you can know God's peace in that tough situation.

3. God can get us through any circumstance.

Not all storms involve clouds, wind, and rain. Sometimes a storm will strike within our family; sometimes emotions will rage at work; occasionally unrest seizes our soul. Yet the truth remains, we can handle whatever comes as long as we depend upon the Lord. The Apostle Paul promised in 1 Corinthians 10:13, "No temptation has seized you except what is common to man. And God is faithful; he will not let you be tempted beyond what you can bear. But when you are tempted, he will also provide a way out so that you can stand up under it." As hard as life may be at times, we can survive any storm with Christ by our side.

Our local paper carried a story some time ago about a couple who served eleven years in prison for intentionally setting a fire that killed their two-year-old son. A further investigation utilizing the latest technology has now determined that the fatal fire was in fact accidental, and all charges have been dropped. But imagine: Jacqueline Latta was thirty years old when she experienced the horrific tragedy of losing her son, and was then arrested and indicted for intentionally taking his life. Amazingly, Jacqueline, who was now 41, expressed no bitterness over being wrongfully imprisoned for one-fourth of her life. Recognizing that everyone is fallible, that people do make mistakes, she said she has chosen to focus on all of the learning and growing that this experience has provided her. She is a person who has made peace with her circumstances.[5]

Shalom means the possession of adequate resources.

I find it interesting that the Hebrew word for peace, *shalom*, means more than silence or the absence of war. It literally means, "the possession of adequate resources." God promises to give us what we need, when we need it. The fruit of His Spirit is peace. His peace then echoes through our lives.

4. Trials help us grow.

This lesson is not a pleasant one. It is unsettling; it may not even seem fair. In fact, sometimes the trials of life are too horrible to even comprehend. But this is not my idea, it is God's. We are told in Romans 5:2b-4, "We rejoice in the hope of the glory of God. Not only so, but we also rejoice in our sufferings, because we know that suffering produces perseverance; perseverance produces character; and character produces hope." When we persevere through difficult circumstances, we can often look back and realize just how much the struggles helped us grow. Wayne Smith, a longtime minister at Southland Christian Church, recently preached the funeral of his brother-in-law, Larry Johnson. During his eulogy Wayne took the time to reminisce about times he had spent with Larry. Wayne said he once rode with Larry from Lexington to Louisville for the National Quartet Convention. Apparently, Larry had a lead foot on the highway. Wayne sat in the front seat and was scared to death. He described that trip down Interstate 64: "I started praying in Versailles. I rededicated my life in Frankfort. I felt a second work of grace in Shelbyville; by the time we arrived at Freedom Hall, I was speaking in tongues!" Now that is vintage "Wayne" humor, but I can tell you, Wayne has also had his share of heartache in life. And he has helped a lot of other people carry theirs. He always says he laughs a lot because he cries a lot. Wayne Smith maintains joy and peace because he trusts God, and he has allowed the trials of

We can all learn and grow from trials. That is part of God's plan for us.

life to make him a better preacher and a better person. We can all learn and grow from trials. That is part of God's plan for us.

5. For the Christian, all troubles are temporary.

This is a critical truth: trials are temporary. I love what it says in 2 Corinthians 4:17-18, "Our light and momentary troubles are achieving for us an eternal glory that far outweighs them all. So we fix our eyes not on what is seen, but on what is unseen. For what is seen is temporary, but what is unseen is eternal." That neighbor next door who is robbing you of peace, that stubborn health condition that has you aching for tranquillity, that coworker who keeps you tied up in knots, that rebellious teenager who is wearing you out, that job that is driving you crazy, that illness the doctor says is terminal, none of it will last. It is all temporary. And if you belong to Christ, the joys of heaven will someday overshadow every hurt, every tear, every heartache of life. Like the old hymn says, "Just one glimpse of Him in glory will the toils of life repay."

"Just one glimpse of Him in glory will the toils of life repay."

The disciples learned a valuable lesson that night on the Sea of Galilee some 2000 years ago: Jesus doesn't prevent storms from coming, but He does have power over them, and He promises to see us through them. It was Augustine who said, "Thou hast made us for Thyself, and our hearts are restless until they find rest in Thee."

The fruit of the Spirit is peace. May it echo loud and clear.

NOTES

[1]William Barclay, *The Gospel of Matthew,* vol. 1, rev. ed. (Philadelphia: Westminster, 1975), p. 316.

[2]Gire, *Moments,* p. 153.

[3]Ibid., p. 154.

[4]Roberta Croteau, editor of *Release* magazine, "Lucky One?" *Aspire* (February/March, 1995).

[5]"Wire Reports," *The Republic,* Aug. 25, 2002.

Reflecting on Lesson Three

1. Why do you think peace is such a challenge in our culture?

2. Can you name a person whom you feel echoes this quality of peace? What is it about him or her that impresses you most?

3. Is there a specific situation that is robbing you of peace? Take a few moments right now to pray that God would enable you to experience His peace despite the pressure.

Consider this:

Have you ever prayed for patience? If so, what happened? Are you easily frustrated? What frustrates you the most? How do you deal with impatience in yourself? in others?

4

ECHOING GOD'S PATIENCE

In this lesson:

- The value of patience
- Helping others with impatience
- Learning to wait on God's timing
- Patience with difficult people

Three stories came out of the opening week of the NFL's 2002-03 season. The Cleveland Browns played the Kansas City Chiefs on that first Sunday. Cleveland led 39-37 with just 3 seconds to go when Cleveland linebacker Dwayne Rudd *thought* he had sacked the quarterback to end the game. In celebration of the play—and the team's victory—Rudd took off his helmet and threw it to the ground. However, just before actually going down, quarterback Trent Green had pitched the ball out to John Tait who ran it for a 36 yard gain. Because Rudd had slammed his helmet, he received a penalty for unsportsman-like conduct, and the Chiefs were granted one final play. With no time on the clock, they kicked a field goal to win the game 40-39. As they say, *"It ain't over till it's over."*[1]

Eric Crouch won the Heisman Trophy as the College Football Player of the Year in 2001. The Wednesday following the opening game of the 2002 season, Crouch retired from pro football, having played all of one game for the St. Louis Rams. Explaining that he had not been able to make the transition from quarterback to wide receiver, he chose to hang it up. Rams Coach Mike Martz said, *"The talent he had, he never gave it a chance."*[2]

Contrast Crouch's story with that of football legend Johnny Unitas who died on September 11, 2002, at the age of 69. Many consider Unitas the greatest quarterback of all time. He completed a record 290 touchdown passes in his career, throwing for at least one touchdown in a record 47 consecutive games. He led the Baltimore Colts to two NFL championships, was named Player of the Decade for the 1960s and the Greatest Player in the First 50 Years of Pro Football. With that kind of incredible career, who would believe that Unitas was only a ninth-round draft pick by the Pittsburgh Steelers in 1955 and was subsequently cut from the team? He signed as a free agent with the Baltimore Colts in '56, and when he finally made his NFL debut in the fourth game of that season, the very first pass of his career was intercepted and returned for a touchdown. He fumbled on his next two possessions. Not exactly a stellar beginning!

The common denominator in each of those stories is patience: a linebacker who couldn't wait until the game was over, a Heisman Trophy winner who expected instant success, and a quarterback who persevered until he got it right. Galatians 5:22-23 reminds us, "The fruit of the Spirit is love, joy, peace, patience, kindness, goodness, faithfulness, gentleness and self-control. Against such things there is no law." The fruit of the Spirit is patience, and yet patience does not come naturally for most 21st-century Americans. We live in a "hurry up" culture. We've got fast food, quick print, glasses in an hour, 30-minute pizza delivery, 10-minute oil changes, and tattoos while you wait. (I didn't know there was any other way to get a tattoo!) One of the reasons I have never bothered using the Internet very much is because I hated to wait for the dial-up connection and for the web pages to download. Now that I have experienced a high-speed DSL connection, I'm hooked. It is hard to wait for things. Max Lucado pointed out that we are the only nation on earth with a mountain called "Rush-More"! And we do![3]

Max Lucado pointed out that we are the only nation on earth with a mountain called "Rush-More"!

Besides the pace at which we live, we are regularly confronted by challenging situations and frustrating people—all tests of our patience. Still further, most of us are not in the habit of taking things as they come; we prefer to *make* things happen! Patience is a tough topic for me to talk about; I am not the most patient person in the world. My wife Gail likes to point out that when I am feeling impatient, I will usually start jiggling my right knee back and forth. When it is really bad, both knees get going! I didn't actually invent One-Hour Photo, but it was invented with me in mind! The problem with preaching on this subject—which I occasionally do—is that there are no simple steps to acquiring this trait. Henry Ward Beecher said, "There's no such thing as preaching patience into people unless the sermon's so long they have to practice it to learn it!" Patience is something we cultivate over time as we mature in our faith, but there are no quick fixes.

And yet, when we give our lives to Christ, the Holy Spirit dwells inside of us; and the Apostle Paul tells us that one of the by-products of God's Spirit is patience. You see, patience is a quality God possesses, and it is something Jesus modeled while He was here on earth; therefore, it is a quality we are promised as well. How exactly can we echo God's patience in the world? Before we look at three snapshots from the life of Christ, let's try to understand what patience really is.

The Greek word for patience used in the New Testament is, *"macrothumos,"* which literally means, *"to take a long time to boil."* The Old Testament Hebrew word suggested more the concept of endurance than simply waiting. It was tied to perseverance. I once heard somebody say that "Patience is idling your motor when you feel like stripping your gears." Patience calls us to face life calmly, even when things don't go our way. Why? Because deep down, we know God is in control. Patience requires us to maintain our composure when we are asked to wait for something we really want or when we are forced to endure something we really dread.

"Patience is idling your motor when you feel like stripping your gears."

Sometimes even the best of friends can test each others' patience. That is what happened in the life of Jesus. Nobody ever modeled this trait better than He did, yet He must have struggled at times. As we consider three interactions Jesus had with His friends Mary and Martha, I think we'll learn some lessons about how we can be patient too.

PATIENT WHEN FEELING PRESSURED

In Luke Chapter 10, Jesus and his disciples stopped by the home of Mary and Martha and their brother Lazarus. Bethany was a bedroom community of Jerusalem, just a little village separated from the hustle and bustle of the big city. Jesus regularly stopped there to see His friends, eat a home-cooked meal, and catch up on the news. Picking up in the middle of verse 39,

> Mary . . . sat at the Lord's feet listening to what he said. But Martha was distracted by all the preparations that had to be made. She came to him and asked, "Lord, don't you care that my sister has left me to do the work by myself? Tell her to help me!"

This is a classic personality clash: the hard-working, serious, highly organized, and easily frustrated Martha stresses over the meal while generous, easy-going, and mild-mannered Mary sits with Jesus, hanging on every word.

Can't you just picture Martha listening to the laughter from the living room while she is cutting up vegetables in the kitchen? "For crying out loud, where's Mary? I thought she was going to toss the salad. And the table hasn't been set, and we've got to wash the silverware, and I needed her to go next door and borrow three eggs. Why isn't she helping me?" As the frustration builds, she is slicing and dicing with a vengeance. Can't you picture her chopping carrots with a meat cleaver? She stomps around for a while, slamming drawers and clanging pots, thinking surely Mary will get the hint and come help her. Nooooo. Finally, she can't take it anymore. She storms into the living room, her apron splattered with gravy, flour on her cheeks, a strand of hair hanging down in her eyes, and says, "Lord, don't you care that my *sister* [she's too mad to call her by name] has left me to do all the work by myself? Tell her how lazy she's being and make her come help me."

Bottom Line: Martha was trying to force her agenda. You see, Jesus and the twelve disciples couldn't very well call ahead to warn Mary, Martha, and Lazarus they were coming. They simply had to drop in unannounced. And don't get me wrong: Martha was glad about it. Seeing Jesus was always a pleasure. However, whipping up a meal for thirteen guests is no small task, especially thirteen men who had been walking around for days and weeks and months, rarely sitting down to a table and eating a home-cooked meal. These guys were hungry, and she felt like only her best would do. Sure she wanted to visit with Jesus, talk over old times, hear the latest news of His ministry, show Him slides of last summer's vacation. But there were potatoes to mash, and gravy to stir, and she had to keep an eye on the meat so it wouldn't dry out, and she didn't want the biscuits to burn. Martha had her hands full. She did not want to disappoint her guests. Take a look at Jesus' response in verse 41, "'Martha, Martha,' the Lord answered, 'You are worried and upset about many things, but only one thing is needed. Mary has chosen what is better, and it will not be taken away from her.'"

Jesus maintained His priorities. Sure the meal was important, and I am confident Martha laid out quite a spread—she was the "Aunt Bea" of Bethany! But life is about more than food. So, despite the pressure to smooth over the situation and keep Martha happy, Jesus used this encounter as a teaching moment to stress the importance of priorities. He reminded Martha that food is temporary, but Mary's choice to listen to Him had eternal implications. I think Jesus was saying, "Workaholics, beware; chronic hurriers, listen closely. There is a

> Workaholics, beware.
> Chronic hurriers,
> listen closely.

time to be busy, and a time to 'be still and know that I am God.' It's all a matter of priorities."

Now, I am in no way suggesting that Mary loved Jesus more than Martha did, or that Mary is the "hero" in this text and Martha's the villain. I am simply suggesting that Mary had her priorities well in line, and Jesus defended her for it. In this particular instance, Martha was out-of-balance. I wonder how Martha responded to Jesus' gentle chiding. Do you think she gladly "took a load off" and sat down at Jesus' feet? Or maybe she begrudgingly sat down, muttering under her breath and pinching Mary when Jesus wasn't looking. Maybe she stomped back into the kitchen, leaving Mary to listen to Jesus all by herself. I like to think that Martha joined Mary, and the two of them together drank in the wisdom that Jesus shared. Then, *together*, they went to the kitchen to finish the meal. And maybe, after supper, James and John cleared the table, and Peter and Andrew took out the trash, and Lazarus washed the dishes and Jesus dried. Maybe Martha got the point that she needed to focus a little more on the really important things. Hopefully, the others got the point that Martha was under a lot of pressure, and they needed to be willing to pitch in and help out as well.

You see, patience does not equal laziness. Jesus was not undermining the importance of work; He was not commending Mary for shirking her duty. He was simply bringing some perspective to the situation. It is *not* wrong to refuse to live life in hyperdrive all the time. It is healthy to force yourself to slow down once in a while. Gail and I like to sit in the backyard in the mornings. She has a cup of coffee, and I have hot chocolate—I'm too young to drink coffee! We have a spot over

A patient person refuses to let the pressures of life take control of his life.

by her flowers, in the shade of a pine tree, where we can sit for a quiet moment before the day begins. We don't get out there every morning, but we do it when we can because it is such a nice way to start the day. A patient person refuses to let the pressures of life take control of his life.

Ultimately, patience means doing the important, not just the urgent. Have you ever heard the concept, "the *tyranny* of the urgent"? It is so easy for the busyness of life to take over. We have to constantly guard against that, and cultivating patience helps do that. Let me give you some suggestions: Drive in the slow lane once in a while, even though you could easily pass that grandma in front of you and cruise through the next light just as it is turning from yellow to red—even though we all know a yellow light means to speed up! Sometimes it is good to slow down. Or how about reading a book to a child—cover-to-cover—even though you are tired and it has been a long day. Or take a walk after supper instead of reading the paper. Or join a weeknight Bible study even though work is wearing you out. Being patient means, rather than simply pushing ourselves toward the destination, we slow down once in a while and experience the journey. That is what Jesus was teaching Martha, and us, that day in Bethany.

PATIENT WITH DIFFICULT TIMING

We discover another key encounter between Jesus and Mary and Martha in John chapter 11. Verse 1 begins, "Now a man named Lazarus was sick. He was from Bethany, the village of Mary and her sister Martha." Verse 3 continues, "So the sisters sent word to Jesus, 'Lord, the one you love is sick.'" It is hard to imagine the fear and anxiety Mary and Martha were going through. And when news like this comes to us—especially when it involves someone we really care about—the natural response is to want to be there with them right away. Loved ones drop everything when a close friend is in serious need. However, verse 6 tells us that when Jesus heard the news, He stayed where He was for two more days. By the time He finally got back to Bethany, Lazarus was already dead and buried. Jesus didn't even make it in time for the funeral.

Mary and Martha wanted Jesus right away, and they naturally assumed He would come on the double. When He did finally show up, Martha said to Him—somewhat accusingly—in verse 21, "Lord, if you had been here, my brother would not have died." Mary said the exact same thing in verse 32. It seems they had talked about this quite a bit. Their expectation wasn't met, and they were both hurt and frustrated.

However, as always, Jesus saw things from God's perspective. He had the ability to see the big picture, and He was willing to wait for God's timing. Consider verse 4, "When he heard this, Jesus said, 'This sickness will not end in death. No, it is for God's glory so that God's Son may be glorified through it.'" Knowing that this event would bring glory to God, Jesus was willing to wait two days before responding to the summons. How do you think He felt during those 48 hours, knowing Mary and Martha were worried sick, that they were grieving desperately once Lazarus had died? On the long trip back to Bethany, what was He feeling? No doubt He wanted to be there—He wanted to give them His peace and strength. But His patience kept His emotions in check.

Now consider verses 38-42,

> Jesus, once more deeply moved, came to the tomb. It was a cave with a stone laid across the entrance. "Take away the stone," he said. "But, Lord," said Martha, the sister of the dead man, "by this time there is a bad odor, for he has been there

four days." Then Jesus said, "Did I not tell you that if you believed, you would see the glory of God?"

And now, verses 43-44,

When he had said this, Jesus called in a loud voice, "Lazarus, come out!" The dead man came out, his hands and feet wrapped with strips of linen, and a cloth around his face. Jesus said to them, "Take off the grave clothes and let him go."

Someone has pointed out that it is a good thing Jesus specified that only Lazarus was to come out of the tomb or the whole cemetery would have come back to life! What an incredible miracle! It is one that Jesus knew was coming, although no one else understood. Even so, verse 35 tells us that "Jesus wept." Despite His power, and His patience, Jesus grieved over the pain of death. Verse 45 reveals the key to His patience: "Therefore many of the Jews who had come to visit Mary, and had seen what Jesus did, put their faith in him." Because Jesus maintained God's perspective, He followed God's schedule rather than that of those around Him. He was able to see the end result, therefore He was patient when the timing became uncomfortable.

He was always doing that. For instance, in John 7, His brothers told Him He ought to go to Jerusalem during the Feast of Tabernacles and make Himself known to the world. They thought it was time for Him to jump-start His public career. Actually, they were skeptical of His identity and wanted to put Him on the spot. Jesus said to them in John 7:8, "You go to the Feast. I am not yet going up to this Feast, because for me the right time has not yet come." From Jesus' arrival, which Scripture says came *"In the fullness of time,"* in other words, "at just the right time," to the timing of His public ministry, of His first miracle, of His crucifixion and resurrection, Jesus always followed God's timetable.

Patience does not equal apathy.

That brings up another important principle: Patience does not equal apathy. When Jesus waited two days before going to see Lazarus, He was not unconcerned—He wasn't just wasting time or shirking His responsibility. He had a greater concern than the obvious one of helping this family He loved, namely, to see more people come to know Him as Lord and Savior. Sometimes patience requires us to wait, even when we want more than anything else to push ahead—even when it makes perfect sense to move forward, and seems foolish to wait. William Barclay wrote, "When our fighting instincts say, 'Go on,' it takes a big and brave man to wait. It is human to fear to miss the chance; but it is great to wait for the time of God—even when it seems like throwing a chance away." We must not try to force the hand of God. He will open the right doors, at the right time, if we are willing to follow Him, at His pace. I once wrestled with a major career move. Following a series of visits and interviews, I returned home to wait for the church to contact me about the position. Because that church was going through a relocation at the time, it took about six weeks for them to get back to me. That was a long and discouraging time of waiting. I wondered what they were thinking. My kids regularly asked if I had heard anything yet. Every time the phone rang, I thought it might be the church. I turned down a couple of other opportunities during that month and a half, hoping that the door would open there eventually. When it did finally open, it became perfectly obvious that that was what God had in mind all along. But waiting can be painful.

All this suggests that patience means active waiting—not passive. I could not just sit around waiting for that church to call. There were sermons to preach, meetings to attend, goals to set, needs to meet, and the future to plan. King David wrote in Psalm

31:15: "O Lord . . . My times are in your hands." If that is true, then maybe—just maybe—that interruption you were forced to endure was not really an unplanned interruption at all; maybe it was a divine appointment that God had in mind all along. Maybe that problem you faced or that delay which caused you such anxiety was all part of God's plan. You may never know for sure. But you are likely to miss opportunities when they do arise unless you are willing to be flexible and trust God's timing. Rather than waiting around for the Lord to do something significant with your life, godly patience suggests that you do the task at hand. And as you are faithful in the little things, He will give you more important things to do.

One of the key principles from the Dale Carnegie course suggests, "Learn to cooperate with the inevitable." Chuck Colson's newsletter for his prison ministry, *Jubilee Extra,* told about a man who did just that. Jackson Buwule is a former prison inmate who battled polio as a child growing up in Uganda and endures a painful deformity today. Jackson came to the United States after high school and got a job in Phoenix, Arizona. However, he wrote a bad check during that time in his life and was sent to prison. There he became a Christian and a dynamic witness for Christ. When he got out, he eagerly anticipated continuing to work in Prison Ministry. Unfortunately, upon his release, the Immigration and Naturalization Service shipped him back to Uganda without even the opportunity to tell his Christian friends what had happened to him. He was devastated by the turn of events. When he finally got word to the Christians in America where he was, it had become obvious he would be in Uganda for quite some time. And yet, as Ron Humphrey explained in the article, "The unscheduled circumstances were no obstacle to ministry for this

"Learn to cooperate with the inevitable."

ex-prisoner." Rather than languishing in Uganda, becoming embittered by the painful separation from his son, Jackson poured his life into ministry there. Understanding the pain, rejection, and isolation that many disabled people experience in Africa, he began a weekly Bible study that has drawn more than 100 disabled participants. He has since conducted programs for the disabled in Kenya as well as Uganda, at the invitation of the government there; he also hosts a Christian radio program. Throughout this challenge to his patience, Jackson insists he carried no grudge against the Americans for sending him back to Uganda. "I broke the law, and I did not convert my green card to U.S. citizenship when I had the chance to do it," he said. "It was all part of a plan greater than any of my own. . . . One day, the INS will allow me to come to America for visits, but now, my work is in Africa."[4] Jackson Buwule is cooperating with the inevitable just as Jesus always did.

PATIENT WHEN FACING CRITICISM

In John chapter 12, we again find Jesus and His disciples visiting Mary and Martha and Lazarus. While there, verse 3 says, "Mary took about a pint of pure nard, an expensive perfume; she poured it on Jesus' feet and wiped his feet with her hair. And the house was filled with the fragrance of the perfume." Simply put, Mary lavished Jesus with love and devotion. And yet, her gesture of worship was neither understood nor appreciated. Instead, the disciples tried to force their perspective on her. Verses 4-5 continue, "One of his disciples, Judas Iscariot, who was later to betray him, objected, 'Why wasn't this perfume sold and the money given to the poor? It was worth a year's wages.'" Matthew makes it clear in his Gospel that Judas was not the only one critical. All the disciples seemed to agree this was a little too lavish; Mary had gone overboard when it came to proper decorum and common sense. However, Jesus corrected their misunderstanding. In verses 7-8 He says, "'Leave her alone,' Jesus replied. 'It was intended that she should save this perfume for the day of my burial. You will always have the poor among you, but you will not always have me.'" Jesus told them to back off. Their critique not only risked hurting Mary's feelings, it was missing the point of her gift. Life is not always about fixing problems and addressing needs. As important as those things are, there comes a time when worshiping Jesus—pouring ourselves into loving Him and seeking Him—is the best thing we can possibly do. And so, Jesus confronted their misguided attitude.

Life is not always about fixing problems and addressing needs.

Please understand, patience does not equal weakness. Jesus was not a pushover. When right and wrong were at stake, and when a beloved follower of His was under attack, He was quick to rise to her defense. I think we can learn a valuable lesson from that: Just because we are patient with people—giving them the benefit of the doubt, accepting their imperfections, and allowing them to make mistakes and then learn from those mistakes—that doesn't suggest that we are weak or lack conviction. Patience is a fruit of the Spirit, and giving people a second chance is godly; but we also need to stand up for biblical values, and sometimes that requires confrontation. Patience requires that we deal with people firmly, but gently. We do not go in with both barrels blazing, blasting anything that moves; but we do take a firm stand for what is right. We choose our timing wisely, and we select our words carefully, but patience never requires that we sweep problems under the rug or refuse to correct those who are clearly out of line. Being patient with people means we want what is best for them, and sometimes that includes calling them on the carpet. The parents of a grown daughter may not be able to forbid her living with her boyfriend; but when she comes home for Christmas, they have every right to insist that she will not sleep with him under their roof. A coworker with a vulgar mouth may require an extra measure of patience; but if he makes unwanted advances, he needs to be reported. New Christians are going to slip back into old patterns of behavior sometimes; they often require patience from their brothers and sisters in Christ as they mature. However, if they start going off the track on spiritual issues, they need to be confronted. It takes wisdom to know when to confront and when to be patient.

Patience is not simply feeling inconvenienced or wishing we could hurry up and get on with life. When people are putting undue pressure on us, when God's timing and our timing don't match up, when we are facing unjust criticism, patience is a challenge. And yet, do you know why patience in those times is so important? Because that is the kind of patience God shows to us. Second Peter 3:9 says, "The Lord is not slow in keeping his promise, as some understand slowness. He is patient with you, not wanting anyone to perish, but everyone to come to repentance." God is patient because He loves us. It is no mistake that the first fruit of the Spirit listed in Galatians is love, and then patience follows shortly thereafter. If we truly love people, we will learn to be patient with them; and if we truly love God, we'll learn to operate according to His timetable. Our patience flows out of our love.

If we truly love people, we will learn to be patient with them; and if we truly love God, we'll learn to operate according to His timetable.

I love the story about a father who was taking his little boy on their first real fishing trip. After ten miles or so in the car, the boy asked, "Daddy, are we almost there?"

"Not yet, son," the father replied.

A few more minutes passed, and the boy asked again, "Daddy, are we almost there?"

Again, daddy answered, "Not yet, son."

Another few minutes passed and the boy asked his question again, so the father explained that they would be in the car at least another hour. He may as well stop asking. The boy waited as long as he could, and finally said, "Daddy, will I still be four years old when we get there?"

When patience proves challenging, it helps to know that we have a Father in the driver's seat who loves us, whose power sustains us, and who knows exactly where we need to go. He never grows tired of our questions, and He promises to get us safely to the final destination. We learn to echo His patience in this busy, fast-paced, often frantic world as we learn to completely trust in Him.

NOTES

[1]*Kansas City Star*, A.P. recap, (Sept. 10, 2002).

[2]*Courier Journal* (Sept. 13, 2002).

[3]Max Lucado, *The Applause of Heaven* (Dallas: Word, 1990), p. 18.

[4]*Jubilee Extra* (Aug. 2002), pp. 2-3.

Reflecting on Lesson Four

1. What kind of situations most often challenge your patience?

2. Do you think your personality more closely resembles that of Mary or Martha in the accounts we considered? Why?

3. What are three tangible things you could do this week to promote a more patient attitude toward life?

Consider this:

Some people seem to be naturally kind, but most of us may always be missing opportunities and saying to ourselves, "If only I had thought to. . . ." Can you remember a situation when you missed an opportunity to show kindness? How can you develop more sensitivity toward the plight of others?

5

ECHOING GOD'S KINDNESS

In this lesson:

- The unnaturalness of kindness
- Balancing kindness and responsibility
- Walking in the shoes of others
- When kindness if demanded

I love Calvin and Hobbes cartoons because there's a little bit of every one of us in the mischievous, six-year-old Calvin. One comic strip shows him chewing a huge wad of bubble gum during class. His teacher, Miss Wormwood, uses the age-old line, "Calvin, do you have enough for everybody?" Struggling to talk with his mouth full, he says, "I think so. But I don't think they'd want it!" Galatians 5:22 tells us, "The fruit of the Spirit is kindness." God's kindness should echo through our lives in order to bless the lives of others. I'm not sure that includes the bubble gum from your mouth, but it does include sharing what you have. Is that all there is to this particular fruit of the Spirit?

As a Christian, is it ever appropriate to say no to a request? Is that being *un*kind? Can a person ever be *too* kind? Sometimes the real kindness is to do for long-term benefit what seems unkind in the short run. And this is only one of the issues that make kindness so tricky.

Back when I preached in Louisville, Kentucky, one particular Tuesday was designated, "Random Acts of Senseless Kindness Day." WHAS Radio suggested that people find various ways to express kindness to others while having no ulterior motive. Put a quarter in somebody's parking meter. Share your umbrella on a rainy day. Let somebody go in front of you at the checkout line. Whoever came up with the idea recognized that we hear enough about senseless crimes and random violence. What we need is more kindness.

From children in the classroom to families in the living room, from coworkers at the office to strangers on the street corner, from candidates during an election to bargain hunters at a yard sale, the world needs more kindness today. "Random Acts of Senseless Kindness" is a good idea, but we need more than that. Kindness is needed every day, not just one day a year. It is needed consistently in relationships, not just at random with strangers; and we ought to perform acts of kindness for a purpose—to meet needs—not just senselessly.

The world needs more kindness today.

Proverbs 11:17 says, "A kind man benefits himself, but a cruel man brings trouble on himself." Ephesians 4:32 insists, "Be kind and compassionate to one another, forgiving each other, just as in Christ God forgave you." And 1 Thessalonians 5:15 adds, "Make sure that nobody pays back wrong for wrong, but always try to be kind to each other." No one ever modeled kindness better than Jesus. Three quick glimpses at three of His miracles will offer some insight when it comes to both cultivating and expressing this fruit in our lives.

KINDNESS OFTEN GOES AGAINST HUMAN NATURE

It is unfortunate but true that kindness proves to run counter to the way many people live. I was at my son Daniel's fifth and sixth-grade football practice one night when, during a scrimmage, I overheard a dad from the other team holler at his son, "Get in there and *punish* somebody!" Now, I'm all for hitting hard in football, but his choice of words struck me as interesting: ***Punish*** *somebody.* We live in a very competitive, dog-eat-dog, "do unto others **before** they do unto you" kind of culture.

A first glimpse of Jesus in Mark 7 shows Him confronted by a desperate woman. His response to her, at first glance, seems anything but kind. However, as always, Jesus knew exactly what He was doing. Mark 7:24-25 recounts,

> Jesus left that place and went to the vicinity of Tyre. He entered a house and did not want anyone to know it; yet he could not keep his presence secret. In fact, as soon as she heard about him, a woman whose little daughter was possessed by an evil spirit came and fell at his feet.

If you have ever had a small child seriously ill, you can begin to relate to how this woman must have felt. It is one thing to have a sick parent, spouse, or friend. That can be both frightening and exasperating. But there is something especially traumatic about the pain of a child. They don't fully understand what is happening to them, we have trouble knowing how to comfort them, and there is the thought—always in the back of your mind—"I wish it were me instead!" Contemporary Christian artist Mark Schultz sings a song of a father praying for his son who is critically ill. The dad concludes by saying, *"He's not just anyone. He's my son."*[1] Schultz captures the agony this woman must have felt for her daughter.

I do not know exactly how this evil spirit came upon the child in our text, or exactly what her symptoms were, but there is no doubt this mother was frantic with concern. Suddenly, in the midst of her desperation, news came that Jesus was in town. By this time, He had gained quite a reputation for His miraculous healings. She knew her nationality was a hindrance, but determined to take the risk anyway. And so she came to the house where He was staying, and she barged in on Him. I don't know how else to put it. He had slipped into town, not really wanting anybody to know He was there. He had been facing opposition in Galilee and needed a break; He wanted an opportunity to be alone with His disciples; He needed some "down" time away from the crowds. Yet, when this woman brought her critical need to Him, Jesus sacrificed His schedule and took time for her.

Kindness may be inconvenient when crises come up at inopportune times.

Immediately, we recognize that kindness may be inconvenient. Let's face it, crises rarely come up at opportune times. It is hard to schedule interruptions. That's the whole point—they interrupt. And when we are stressed out or worn out, it just gets tougher. Our thoughts typically turn inward when our emotional resources are depleted. Yet, Jesus focused on others, even when it would seem only natural for Him to be thinking about Himself—even when He must have felt "used up." How can we cultivate that kind of attitude? The Golden Rule says, "Do unto others as you would have them do unto you." Rather than reacting when a need arises or when we are interrupted, it might help to stop and ask ourselves, "How would I like to be treated in this situation? How would I want someone to minister to me if I were in his shoes? What *would* Jesus do?"

Maybe we should evaluate what would make us feel loved and valued at a given moment, and then do that for someone else instead. Husbands, it might mean we fix a soft drink or a meal for our wives when we wish they would do it for us. Wives, it might mean you go to your husband's softball games once in a while so you can watch his inglorious attempt at reliving his glory days! For all of us it might mean doing a job around the house that we wish somebody else would take care of, or serving at church in an area that gets little recognition. The whole concept of "servant leadership" is that we never say, "That's not in my job description," but rather, when we see a need, we meet it. This woman's interruption, while understandable, was not what Jesus had in mind; yet He was still kind to her.

Look at what James wrote in 2:15-17,

> Suppose a brother or sister is without clothes and daily food. If one of you says to him, "Go, I wish you well; keep warm and well fed," but does nothing about his physical needs, what good is it? In the same way, faith by itself, if it is not accompanied by action, is dead.

When we see a need, we ought to help. However, the Apostle Paul clarified in 2 Thessalonians 3:10, "For even when we

When we see a need, we ought to help.

When in doubt, it is always better to err on the side of generosity.

were with you, we gave you this rule: 'If a man will not work, he shall not eat.'" Kindness does not mean we foolishly give money to every person who sticks his hand out. People need to be taught responsibility—and a strong work ethic—and it is not good stewardship to carelessly give to those who are taking advantage. But having said that, it also needs to be pointed out that when we are in doubt whether the need is legitimate, it is always better to err on the side of generosity. First Corinthians 6:7 reminds us that it is always better to be wronged and cheated than to cheat and do wrong. Sometimes kindness is inconvenient—even uncomfortable—but it is still vital to demonstrate.

Kindness also forces us to overcome barriers. Verses 26-30 say, "The woman was a Greek, born in Syrian Phoenicia." In other words, she was a Gentile.

> She begged Jesus to drive the demon out of her daughter. "First let the children eat all they want," he told her, "for it is not right to take the children's bread and toss it to their dogs." "Yes, Lord," she replied, "but even the dogs under the table eat the children's crumbs." Then he told her, "For such a reply, you may go; the demon has left your daughter." She went home and found her child lying on the bed, and the demon gone.

What on earth did Jesus mean concerning not taking the children's bread and giving it to their "dogs"? The Jews in ancient Palestine often referred to Gentiles as "dogs," so Jesus was pointing out that His ministry was to the "children" first—the Jews—not to Gentile "dogs" like she happened to be.

I don't know about you, but this looks to me like a dramatic example of *unkindness* rather than kindness. Why would Jesus talk to her this way? As I studied this text, I learned that the word Jesus used here for "dog" was not the customary one. While the Jews often used a term for Gentiles that denoted the wild dogs of the streets, Jesus used a word that referred to a house dog, a beloved pet. I realize that is still not exactly a compliment, but Jesus was intentionally using a play on words. You see, it is likely this woman expected Him to ignore her or even mistreat her. That would have been the typical response. However, she had heard there was something different about Jesus—and her daughter's situation *was* desperate—so she decided to take the chance. Well, Jesus did respond in a way similar to that of other Jews she had met, and yet His choice of words—and no doubt, the tone of His voice—gave her hope. When she answered, "But even the dogs under the table eat the children's crumbs," her response suggested that she had picked up on His word play. She realized He had chosen that word very specifically. Her reply also demonstrated perseverance and faith. And so, with a smile on His face and a twinkle in His eyes, Jesus met her need. She went home and found her little girl miraculously healed. It was true, He had come to minister to the Jews first, but not to the Jews only. Jesus responded to this woman's need with compassion and kindness; He saw past their differences and met her at the point of her need.

The church should be the first place where the Spirit of God breaks down barriers such as racial discord and prejudice. When people are in Christ and filled with His Spirit, racial distinctions become irrelevant. Galatians 3:28, "There is neither Jew nor Greek, slave nor free, male nor female, for you are all one in Christ Jesus." More than anyone else, Christians should demonstrate

The church should be the first place where the Spirit breaks down barriers of racial discord and prejudice.

to the world that the love of Christ is bigger than man's biases and hostilities. And so, this first glimpse of Christ's kindness includes a reminder that we treat people who are different from us with dignity and respect, even when it is inconvenient.

KINDNESS BEGINS WITH TRUE EMPATHY

It is vital for us to grasp what others are really going through if we are going to show them Christlike kindness and compassion. Mark 7 offers us another glimpse of Jesus' incredible kindness. Verses 31-32 explain,

> Then Jesus left the vicinity of Tyre and went through Sidon, down to the Sea of Galilee and into the region of the Decapolis. There some people brought to him a man who was deaf and could hardly talk, and they begged him to place his hand on the man.

Helen Keller once said that if she had a choice between being blind or being deaf, she would choose to be blind. Blindness cuts you off from things, but deafness alienates you from people. This man in our text may have been intelligent, he may have had a great personality, but his disability cut him off from most relationships. In that day, it is likely that he had never learned to read or write, and any sign language he used would have been primitive at best. He lived in a world all to himself. Yet, Jesus was sensitive to how he felt.

In fact, this is another important lesson: Kindness protects the feelings of others. Verse 33 says, "After he took him aside, away from the crowd, Jesus put his fingers into the man's ears. Then he spit and touched the man's tongue." Jesus took him aside. He understood that the man was probably uncomfortable—that he felt like he was on display—so, rather than "grandstand" the miracle by making a scene, He sought to protect the man's privacy by stepping out of the limelight; He refused to make a spectacle of him just to gain an audience. Jesus did not always heal in private. There were times when miracles were done right out in the open—they were intentionally done to demonstrate His deity. But Jesus was so sensitive to this man—so in touch with his feelings—that He did it differently this time. Football coach Dan Reeves once said, *"You can tell the character of a man by the way he treats those who can do nothing for him."* Jesus' character shines through clearly in his dealings with this man.

He also showed sensitivity to the man's feelings by communicating with him in a way he could understand. Rather than using words—which the man could not hear—Jesus touched him. Even though it sounds kind of disgusting to us, Jesus spit onto His finger and touched the man's tongue. Apparently, in ancient times, saliva was thought to have curative power. When Jesus did this, it became clear to the deaf man that Jesus was about to perform a miracle. For the first time in ages, hope probably welled up inside of him. Was it possible that the long years of silence were about to be broken?

We learn another important truth even before Jesus healed this man: Kindness feels the pain of others. That is what empathy is all about. Consider at verse 34, "Jesus looked up to heaven and with a deep sigh said to him, 'Ephphatha!' (which means, 'Be opened!')." Jesus looked up to heaven to demonstrate the source of His power, and then He sighed—in fact, the text stresses that He sighed deeply. Why did He sigh? It is only speculation, but I think, seeing this man's need, Jesus was suddenly overwhelmed by the suffering of the world. It confronted Him in the faces of His audience everyday, and yet something about this man reminded Jesus in a pow-

Kindness feels the pain of others.

erful way just how much a gentle touch, an act of mercy, and a few kind words were so desperately needed by those He had come to save.

We live in a hurting world. I once heard a preacher say, "When you're preaching, remember there is a broken heart in every pew." People who are kind have the ability to feel others' pain. They put themselves in other peoples' shoes and identify with the hurt. That is why they are so eager to do something to help. On the other hand, people who are unkind lack the ability—or have squelched the ability—to relate to the hurts of others. They don't think about anyone but themselves.

As we look at how Jesus turned this man's life around, we are reminded that kindness compels us to help when we can. Verse 35, "At this, the man's ears were opened, his tongue was loosened and he began to speak plainly." Jesus spoke but a single command: "Ephphatha—Be opened." Immediately, the man could both hear *and* speak! The words he had longed to say came tumbling out of his mouth. The sounds he had only imagined suddenly registered in his brain: music, laughter, a whispered conversation, dogs barking, birds singing, crickets chirping, teaching in the synagogue, the words, "I love you." All were available to him following one moment of kindness from the Savior.

Now, you may be thinking: "I would love to be able to do that! If only I could miraculously heal people, I would be kind to everybody. Forget about holding a 'Healing Crusade' at the Convention Center, I would just go to the hospital and start emptying beds!" Remember what Jesus said: Be faithful with a little, and then I'll give you more responsibility. If you aren't being kind to people now—with the gifts you already have—it is not likely you would be kind if you had a miraculous spiritual gift. We may never be able to touch a deaf man and heal him instantaneously, but we can all show that man kindness. We can treat him with respect, try to understand his needs, and do all we can to integrate him into God's family even though he has a disability. We can put ourselves in his place and respond to him in a way that shows him honor. Empathy is a key component of kindness.

One Friday last spring the severe weather sirens went off in our town, and all of the elementary school children had to go out in the hallway, get down on their knees, and cover their heads. My daughter MacKenzie, who was in fourth grade at the time, said that some of the kids in her area were pretty scared that Friday, and some of the girls were crying. So her teacher, Mark Yeaton, rather than hollering at the students to be quiet, went back to the classroom and got his guitar. He came back and played music for them. He led them in a game of "Name That Tune." I'm not sure, but I wonder if maybe he remembered what it was like to be a kid and to hear that there was a tornado warning and wonder if you are about to be blown away, and to be so scared you can hardly stand it. Maybe he remembered just enough to know that the kids, in that moment, needed a little comfort and distraction rather than threats and discipline. Kindness empathizes.

KINDNESS REQUIRES PERSEVERANCE

There is one more glimpse of Jesus we don't want to overlook: Mark 8:1-3,

> During those days another large crowd gathered. Since they had nothing to eat, Jesus called his disciples to him and said, "I have compassion for these people; they have already been with me three days and have nothing to eat. If I send them home hungry, they will collapse on the way, because some of them have come a long distance."

The crowd had been with Jesus for three days, listening to Him preach and watching Him heal the sick. If they had brought any food at all, by now it was long gone. They were hungry, and Jesus wanted to feed them. The disciples, possibly in a patronizing tone of voice, explained to Jesus that there was no possible way to provide a meal for so many people. Where could they possibly find enough food in such a remote place? So Jesus asked, "What do you have to offer them?" They managed to scrounge up seven loaves of bread and a few small fish. Satisfied, Jesus instructed the crowd to sit down, He blessed the food, the disciples passed it out, and miraculously, some 4,000-plus people got a free lunch.

Two quick thoughts come to mind concerning this miracle as it pertains to kindness, and our need to persevere. One is that kindness is often mundane. It is one thing for a celebrity to visit an orphanage or a cancer ward when the cameras are rolling. It is another thing to serve a meal at a homeless shelter, stop to help somebody change a flat tire, or pick up groceries for a shut-in when nobody is there to see or to applaud. William Barclay suggested that consideration, or kindness, is a "*virtue which never forgets the details of life.*"[2] A hungry crowd is not a very exciting need. It is not nearly as dramatic as a frantic mother with a demon-possessed child, or a deaf man who cannot speak. Sometimes it is easier to be kind when the need is desperate. When there is a flood or hurricane, communities often rally to the occasion—at least, at first. When a family suffers a tragic death, the outpouring of love is often overwhelming—for a while. The number of blood donations following the 9/11 attacks was enormous; however, blood banks are once again begging for donors. I'm not disputing that kindness is essential in times of crisis. But I won-

Kindness is often mundane.

der how eager we are to help those who face ordinary, run-of-the-mill needs?

The *Courier Journal* carried an article by columnist Cal Thomas several years ago entitled, "More Than Politics."[3] He wrote, "We [in America] suffer not from a failure of political organization or power, but a failure of love. . . . The way to transform a nation is not by politics alone. It is not enough to support a welfare reform bill. We must also mentor the children of poverty who live without fathers and without hope. It is not enough to fight the gay rights lobby. We must comfort AIDS patients preparing for a lonely death. It is not enough to support a constitutional amendment banning abortion. We must . . . provide young women in trouble with a home and a sympathetic ear." Kindness applies to everyday, mundane needs as well as the huge, once-in-a-lifetime emergencies. Mr. Thomas said, on another occasion, "Love talked about is easily ignored. Love demonstrated is irresistible."

"Love talked about is easily ignored. Love demonstrated is irresistible."

This final lesson pertaining to kindness reminds us that it must be ongoing in nature. This miracle in Mark 8 is known as the feeding of the 4,000. Just two chapters back, in Mark 6, we read about the feeding of the 5,000 that Jesus managed with five loaves and two fish. Hunger was a need that would not go away. This was not like the deaf man suddenly regaining his hearing, or the little girl being delivered from the power of a demon. Their problems were gone for good. This crowd would be hungry again in a matter of hours. It was a need that couldn't be resolved with one meal.

Often, the reward for kindness is another request for kindness. If we do something nice for someone, they often come

> Often, the reward for kindness is another request for kindness.

back and ask again. If you give to a charity one year, they don't say the next year, "Mr. Jones helped us last year, we won't bother him this year." They don't call and say, "You gave twenty dollars last year, would you consider giving ten this year?" You know as well as I do, they come back, and they hope for more the next time. The real test of kindness comes in the repeat performance. We have to be willing to keep stepping in, keep helping out, and keep meeting needs.

Incidentally, there are times when we have to allow people to do for themselves, even if they struggle. We can do more harm than good by continuing to bail people out of every difficult situation and refusing to allow them to grow up and stand on their own two feet. Sometimes the kindest thing we can do is say "No." Jesus fed the 5,000 after a single afternoon. He didn't feed the 4,000 until they had been with Him for three days. He did not come to earth just to feed large crowds. His fundamental purpose was not "A chicken in every pot," or a perpetual welfare program, or even an end to world hunger. He came as the Bread of Life to teach us what true nourishment—spiritual nourishment—is all about, and to ultimately save us from our sins. But along the way, He showed us that kindness is mandatory, even if it is inconvenient; that we must learn to empathize with others, even those different from ourselves; and that kindness—like love—always perseveres. It never fails.

Acts of kindness are not usually earth-shattering events that make the front page of the paper or the lead story on the news. We are talking about treating people the way Jesus did. We are talking about letting God's Spirit shine out of us to brighten the lives of those we come into contact with everyday. We are simply talking about echoing the kindness of God. In traffic, if someone needs to get in, let him in. In church, if someone needs to sit down, move over. At work, if someone needs help in another department, help if you can. At a restaurant, if someone spills a drink, dodge it, and then lend a hand to clean it up. At home, I've heard it said: "If you wear it, hang it up; if you drop it, pick it up; if it rings, answer it; if it howls, feed it." How often have you heard the old line, "People don't care how much you know until they know how much you care"?

Tom Bodett provides the familiar voice on the Motel 6 commercials that assures us: "We'll leave the light on for you." In his book, *As Far As You Can Go without a Passport*, he tells about his Grandma Hatty. Tom's mother grew up during the Depression, working hard at the dairy that his grandma and grandpa owned. They lived near the train tracks, and because it was the Depression, hoboes regularly came by looking for handouts as they made their way to nowhere in particular. Grandma Hatty was glad to share what little they had, but she always made sure the "bums" as she called them washed milk cans, shoveled snow, or did something helpful to earn their meal. Apparently, Hatty's family got to be pretty popular on the hobo circuit.

In fact, the hoboes had a practice of scratching a white X with chalk on the gateposts of those houses where a guy could get a handout. It was supposed to be a secret sign, but Grandma Hatty knew it was there. She never paid much attention to that mark, except once. It was the Sunday before Christmas, and on the way in from church, Hatty noticed that a rainstorm the day before had washed the chalk off the post out front. It turned cold right away, and the snow piled up during the afternoon. Grandma and Grandpa sat in the front room watching hoboes trudge past the house, but none of them were stopping. Suddenly, it hit her—the white X was gone.

Now, some people might have been glad to have a little peace and quiet on the Sunday before Christmas, but not Grandma Hatty. She slipped on her overcoat, hiked out to the gate, and put a huge white X on the post that nobody could possibly miss. Tom Bodett ended his story by saying, "I don't know what all this means except that in this hard-hearted world we live in, we should all have a gatepost out front, and . . . go out and put a great big white X on that thing."[4]

Jesus' feeding of the 4,000 and the 5,000, His healings, even His turning water to wine, all echo God's provision for us from the very beginning of creation through this very day. Likewise that echo reverberates in our acts of kindness to each other in even the smallest of deeds.

NOTES

[1]Mark Schultz, "He's My Son."

[2]William Barclay, *The Gospel of Mark, rev. ed.* (Philadelphia: Westminster, 1975), p. 182.

[3]Cal Thomas, "More Than Politics," *Courier Journal* (March 22, 1995).

[4]Tom Bodett, *As Far As You Can Go without a Passport* (Reading, MA: Addison-Wesley, 1985), pp. 47-50.

Reflecting on Lesson Five

1. Who is the kindest person you know? Describe a time when he or she communicated that kindness to you.

2. What examples from the life of Jesus most clearly demonstrate kindness?

3. Can you think of one person to whom you need to show kindness? What can you do today to express kindness to him or her?

Consider this:

Ever been called a "goody-two-shoes?" How did that make you feel? Did you want to misbehave to prove the name did not fit? Imagine how Jesus might have handled such criticisms as a teenager. Be prepared to share you thoughts.

6

ECHOING GOD'S GOODNESS

In this lesson:

- What is goodness?
- Threats to our goodness
- Jesus' teachings on goodness
- Preservation of goodness

Have you ever stopped to consider how quickly you can ruin your reputation? On a recent Saturday afternoon, as I was leaving the church office, a father and son stopped me looking for a birthday party that was supposed to be held at our church. The invitation said Fifth and Lafayette, but we figured out he actually needed the Youth Center at Fourth and Lafayette. About the time we got him headed in the right direction, I met another family who was also looking for the birthday party. I got them situated and then got into the car to head home. As I drove around the block, I saw another mom walking with her son who looked to be about the same age as the kids I had just met; she was looking at a piece of paper, so I assumed she was lost too.

I pulled over, rolled my window down, and said, "Ma'am, are you looking for a party?" She looked at me kind of funny, and said, "No." I immediately said, "Oh, I meant a kids' birthday party!" and I stumbled all over myself trying to explain what I really intended to say. Can't you just see the headlines: "Local minister 'hits' on mom as she takes walk with her son!" It is amazing how quickly you can ruin your reputation!

The Apostle Paul said the Fruit of the Spirit is goodness. However, that is not an easy attribute to describe or define. We use the word for everything from a good dog to a good hot dog—a good meal to a good cry to a good person. What did Paul mean, "The fruit of the Spirit—the result of the Holy Spirit's presence in our lives—is goodness"? We have already talked about being kind and patient and loving; in the next couple of chapters, we will look at faithfulness and self-control. Goodness must be something different. I would suggest to you that goodness is moral integrity, obedience to God's will, and submission to His authority. Goodness is about who we are on the inside, and how we behave outwardly. If you have children, you understand that goodness is based on behavior. Once children learn to be compliant and obedient, how do people often describe them? They say, "He's a good boy." "She sure is being good." As people

Goodness is moral integrity, obedience to God's will, and submission to His authority.

mature, we begin to use words like character and integrity, but the meaning is still the same: Those people are "good."

Again in this chapter, let's look to Jesus as our perfect model. Acts 10:38 says, "God anointed Jesus of Nazareth with the Holy Spirit and . . . He went around doing good." Because He personified goodness, and because these attributes of His are to echo through our lives, we share a similar goal: doing good through the power of God's Spirit. However, as was the case with Jesus, Satan doesn't want us to do good, or to be good. He is going to do anything within his power to deter us from this goal.

TEMPTATION UNDERMINES GOODNESS

When Jesus was about 30 years old, He left Nazareth—the carpenter's shop, His family and friends—and went straight to the Jordan River where His cousin John the Baptist was preaching and baptizing people. When Jesus expressed His desire to be baptized, John questioned the necessity. Jesus insisted, so John agreed. When He came up out of the water, as a sign of affirmation from God, Luke tells us the Holy Spirit descended on Jesus like a dove, and a voice from heaven proudly proclaimed, "You are my Son whom I love. With You I am well pleased."

What a great way to begin ministry: baptized by John, ordained by God, and anointed by the Holy Spirit. Jesus was ready to go out and change the world. But it was not that easy. Before His ministry began, Jesus was tested. How good was He? How good would He be under pressure? The Spirit led Jesus out to a desert area, and there Satan tested His goodness. Luke 4:1-2, "Jesus, full of the Holy Spirit, returned from the Jordan and was led by the Spirit in the desert, where for forty days he was tempted by the devil. He ate nothing during those days, and at the end of them he was hungry." After forty days, I'll say He was hungry! My kids are usually hungry in 40 minutes! In Satan's first recorded words to Jesus, we immediately see some common characteristics of temptation.

1. Satan challenges our identity.

Verse 3 begins, "The devil said to him, '*If* you are the Son of God. . . .'" Satan knew very well that Jesus was the Son of God. There was no question about it. However, Jesus was so weak from the forty days of fasting, and that voice from heaven and the supernatural dove at His baptism were such distant memories, the devil figured he could easily use that one little word, "if" like a chisel to chip away at Jesus' resolve. Not "because you are the Son of God," but *"if."* He thought he might plant just a few seeds of doubt in the Lord's mind. "*Sure*, you're the Son of God—out here starving in the desert. Why, look at you, nothing but skin and bones. Who's going to believe you came from heaven?" Satan tried that tactic with Jesus, and frankly, he does it with us too.

Please understand, Satan himself went after Jesus because Jesus was the primary threat to Satan's kingdom of destruction. However, Satan is not omnipresent like God. He cannot be everywhere at once. He cannot tempt everybody at once. To be honest, you and I are not nearly as much of a threat to the devil as Jesus was, so he does not usually personally come after us. Saying that Satan tempts everybody is like saying Adolf Hitler killed 6 million Jews during World War II. What we mean is that Hitler's Nazi forces killed those people. Satan himself may not come after each of us per-

> Satan himself may not come after each of us personally, but his demonic forces are responsible.

sonally, but his demonic forces are responsible for much of the evil and much of the temptation in the world. His name is used to personify his power over his host of demons.

So let me ask you: Does Satan ever try this kind of temptation with you, challenging your identity? "You call yourself a Christian? Why, you couldn't belong to God's family and act the way you do. You must not really be 'saved' after all." Satan wants us to lack confidence as children of God. He tries to confuse the issues and make us doubt our security in Christ. He dredges up past failures—he points his finger with such scalpel-like precision—that we start to wonder if maybe we are just fooling ourselves with all this talk of hope, assurance, and salvation. "You know, maybe he's right. How could God forgive a guy like me?" I have heard Dave Stone, minister and author, say, "The next time Satan reminds you of your past, remind him of *his* future." Despite the cleverness of his arguments, Satan is just doing what he does best—deceive.

2. Satan knows our areas of vulnerability.

Remember what verse 2 of Luke 4 said? "For forty days he was tempted by the devil." These three examples in Luke are only a cross section of what was nearly six weeks of constant bombardment. These were chosen because they summarize the main areas of temptation we all face at one time or another, what the Apostle John refers to as the lust of the flesh, the lust of the eyes, and the pride of life. We might put it even more simply: lust, greed, and pride. The three temptations here demonstrate Satan's understanding of man's vulnerability. Why did he encourage Jesus to turn stones into bread? Because Jesus had been fasting for 40 days. Why encourage Jesus to bow down and worship him? Because the Lord had been living in poverty, having abandoned the splendors of heaven. The instant wealth Satan promised may have looked pretty good right about then. Why expect Jesus to throw Himself off the highest point of the Temple? Because Jesus was just about to launch His public ministry, and the instant fame and acclaim He would have acquired from having the angels catch Him would have propelled Him to the status of pop legend.

Now maybe turning stones into bread would not have been the biggest temptation for you. If you are like me, maybe it would have been more tempting to turn the stones into mint chocolate chip ice cream! You see, temptation does not come to everyone the same way. What tempts you might not tempt me. For some people, the longing for alcohol is not just a day-by-day battle but a minute-by-minute, full-blown war. Frankly, I don't understand much about that struggle because I have never been tempted toward alcoholism. Satan does not bother going after me in that way. Similarly, holding grudges is not a real problem for me. I have a quick temper, but it usually cools down right away, and I am pretty quick to forgive. But I do understand lust. I understand greed. I understand selfishness. Satan knows how to get to me, and he knows how to get to you, too.

Temptation does not come to everyone the same way.

Chuck Swindoll compared temptation to a fisherman choosing bait from his tackle box. He said, "Our enemy, crafty and clever and experienced as he is, knows which lure best attracts each one of us."[1] Satan and his demons can make the most destructive behavior appear attractive. They are masters at utilizing the power of suggestion. They may take an innocent hug from a friend of the opposite sex and plant the seed of arousal. They may take our next-door neighbor's new car and plant a seed of envy. Or maybe tax time gives them the opportunity to plant a seed of dishonesty. Then there is that tender spot on your elbow that you can bump into something and suddenly come up with all kinds of colorful vocabulary words. Satan wants nothing more than to distract us from honoring God. He is the master of temptation.

Satan wants nothing more than to distract us from honoring God.

3. Satan tries to rationalize immorality.

One of the most unnerving things about this text is that Satan quoted Scripture in verses 9-11 of Luke 4.

> The devil led him to Jerusalem and had him stand on the highest point of the temple. "If you are the Son of God," he said, "throw yourself down from here. For it is written: 'He will command his angels concerning you to guard you carefully; they will lift you up in their hands, so that you will not strike your foot against a stone.'"

Now, wait a minute! I thought the Bible was our weapon. What is the devil doing using it? He uses it to convince us that the evil we want to do is not so bad. Not only does he make sinful behavior appealing, he helps us figure out a way to justify it.

I read an article in the Religion Section of our local newspaper on cohabitation. In light of our country's skyrocketing statistics of couples living together without being married, the article quoted several local ministers who lovingly but firmly admonish couples to live separately until they tie the knot. However, one local pastor from the Unitarian Church actually encourages cohabitation, explaining to the couples she counsels that she and her husband lived together before they got married: "It makes logical sense," she insists.[2] Satan is using that kind of mind-set to lead countless couples into a sinful lifestyle.

There are certainly other rationalizations. One person uses the assurance of God's love to prove no possibility exists that anyone will ever really go to hell. They contend that a loving God would never do that. Another person uses the Bible's teaching on judgment and hell to prove there is no such thing as a loving God. The truth is, Satan knows just enough Scripture to twist God's truth to his advantage. He often convinces us that the sin we are enticed by is not really wrong or it is only a one-time thing or is simply no big deal. Despite this full-blown frontal attack by the devil, let's consider the character Jesus displayed.

Satan knows just enough Scripture to twist God's truth to his advantage.

JESUS EXEMPLIFIES GOODNESS

Hebrews 4:15 reminds us, "We do not have a high priest who is unable to sympathize with our weaknesses, but we have one who has been tempted in every way, just as we are--yet was without sin." Jesus was tempted in *every* way. Even so, He squarely faced the enemy, and He did it over and over again while here on earth. I've read the writings of Bible scholars which suggest that, because Jesus was God, He was incapable of sin. I don't believe that at all. Jesus was fully God, but He was God *in the flesh.* He was a human being. The very reason His victory over temptation is so meaningful is because He was just as capable of sin as the rest of us. The reason He sympathizes with our weaknesses is because He understands the pressure of sin's appeal. Here, Jesus courageously, defiantly, stood His ground and maintained His goodness. Despite His weakened condition, He stood toe-to-toe with Satan and won. Forty days of temptation and not a single misstep. Forty days of fasting, and not a single lapse in His character. Jesus stood up to the devil, and Satan blinked first. The Bible says in James 4:7, "Submit yourselves, then, to God. Resist the devil, and he will flee from you." That's what Jesus did.

Jesus also quoted God's Word proficiently. He said in Luke 4:4, "It is written: 'Man does not live on bread alone.'" In verse 8, "It is written: 'Worship the Lord your God and serve him only.'" And in verse 12, "It says: 'Do not put the Lord your God to the test.'" Each time Satan tempted Jesus, He responded with a verse of Scripture. He used God's Word with precision and skill.

I remember when I was little, and we would have a time in Sunday School to each quote a Bible verse, invariably somebody would try to use John 11:35, the shortest verse in the Bible. "Jesus wept." Only, they would get mixed up and say, *"God wept."* And to further complicate things, they had no idea what "wept" meant! Two words, they would get half of them wrong, and they couldn't define the other half! Jesus wielded God's Word as a powerful weapon against Satan. The Bible itself says God's Word is living and active, sharper than a double-edged sword. Jesus used God's Word to help Him maintain His integrity.

Still further, we see that He focused on His main priority. Had Jesus gone through with this "jump off the Temple" stunt, He might have gathered a crowd, but not for the right reason. He wouldn't have been perceived as a Savior, but a novelty—a stuntman—sort of a "*Good* Knievel!" Satan was tempting Jesus to step off the Temple and abandon His true mission. However, Jesus had come to seek and save the lost, not gather a crowd. He'd come to build a kingdom, not entertain an audience. And so, again in verse 12, He says, "Do not put the Lord your God to the test." Don't miss what He said. He told Satan not to try to test the Lord God. He was very clearly stating that He was God, and that Satan was not to test Him. Understanding His true identity, He refused to abandon His purpose. Jesus stood up to Satan and overcame the temptations laid before Him. Why? Because He was good! The question remains, how can we do that?

> Jesus had come to build a kingdom, not entertain an audience.

CHRISTIANS PRACTICE GOODNESS

I love the story about the preacher who was trying to lose some weight, so he swore off of red meat, potato chips, and all sweets. One morning, he came into the office carrying a box of chocolate donuts. His secretary said, "I thought you were on a diet."

He said, "I am, but the Lord *wanted* me to buy these donuts."

"Oh really?"

"Yeah, I was on the way to the office, and I knew I'd pass the bakery, so I prayed, 'Lord, if you want me to buy a dozen donuts this morning, then please let there be a parking space open right in front of the bakery.' Sure enough, on my *eighth* trip around the block, there was a parking place, right in front of the bakery!" When we face the temptations of life, how can we make goodness echo in our behavior?

1. We find strength in Christ.

Hebrews 2:18, "Because [Jesus] himself suffered when he was tempted, he is able to help those who are being tempted." Often, we bail out when it comes to character because we have already given up hope before the battle even begins; we have already decided we don't have what it takes to succeed. Hebrews tells us that because Jesus understands temptation—because He has been there—He will give us the strength we need. However, we have to long for character; we have to pray daily for the strength to overcome. Jesus will help, but we have to ask!

2. We immerse ourselves in God's Word.

King David wrote in Psalm 119:11, "I have hidden your word in my heart that I might not sin against you." It is not enough to have God's Word on the coffee table; we need to have it in our hearts. When I first went to preach in Louisville, Kentucky, Dale DeNeal was the youth minister. Dale led a very special week of church camp one summer for high school students at White Mills Christian Camp. The whole week dealt with spiritual warfare, and on opening night, he gave each camper one of those gold-colored plastic swords—a child's toy. For the next seven days, that sword was to represent God's Word, what the Apostle Paul referred to in Ephesians as the "Sword of the Spirit." Throughout the week, the campers were required to have their swords with them at all times: while they played sports, while they ate and slept, even in the shower. Several of the faculty members carried paint-ball guns, which represented the "flaming darts of the evil one." Whenever one of these "representatives of Satan" would aim his gun at a camper, the student had about 5 seconds to quote a verse of Scripture. If he could not think of one, he was shot. The entire exercise served to teach this principle: God's Word is fundamental to overcoming temptation, but we have to know it. A pastor friend of mine wrote in the front of his Bible, "God's Word will keep me from sin, or sin will keep me from God's Word." We have to decide which it is going to be.

God's Word is fundamental to overcoming temptation, but we have to know it.

3. We build some accountability into our lives.

Most of us struggle with accountability because, deep down, we don't want anybody to know who we really are. We are afraid people would be turned off—even repulsed—if they knew what we were really like on the inside. But we need fellow Christians who can come alongside us and help us stay strong. James 5:16 says, "Therefore confess your sins to each other and pray for each other so that you may be healed." I have heard that the one common denominator among preachers who have committed sexual immorality and destroyed their character is that they had no accountability in their lives. Nobody was holding their feet to the fire and helping them stay straight. We need one or two friends of the same sex to whom we can open up about our struggles, those who will ask us the hard questions and keep us on the right path.

4. We consider the devastating consequences of immorality.

For instance, before you go out and cheat on your spouse, before you throw your integrity away on a one-night stand, before you squander the years you've spent building your character, ask yourself what you are going to say to your wife when she finds out you have been unfaithful. Think about what it is going to feel like trying to explain to your son or daughter why you are moving out. Consider how it will be when your friends at church find out you have committed adultery. Numbers 32:23 states, "Be sure that your sin will find you out." Sometimes we sin and get away with it for a while. But it will come out sometime. Before you take the risk, consider the devastating consequences.

Sometimes we sin and get away with it for a while.

Garrison Keillor, in one of his *News from Lake Woebegone* stories, told about a man named Jim who considered an affair with a coworker of his. He was headed down the path of immorality until he thought through the consequences. He finally realized, *"While I thought my sin would be secret, I realized it would be no more secret than an earthquake!"* No more secret and far more devastating.

5. We remember that failure need not be final.

First John 1:9 reminds us, "If we confess our sins, he is faithful and just and will forgive us our sins and purify us from all unrighteousness." Maybe you have totally trashed your character. Maybe you have really blown it, not just privately but publicly, and you are wondering if you can ever recover your reputation. I cannot guarantee that the fickle crowds will trust you again. I can't promise that you will not have some serious consequences in the future from your failure in the past. But God promises that, if you really want to be forgiven, and you are willing to change, He is eager to forgive. We need to get beyond the excuse that we are only human and sin is just part of our nature. We need to stop rationalizing our stubborn rebellion. Granted, we are not perfect, at least not in this life. But if we are willing to get serious about building consistent character into our lives—truly being good—God is ready to help us do that. Jesus is ready, not only to model perfect goodness, but to help cultivate it in us.

When I was a freshman at Cincinnati Bible College, then President Harvey Bream shared a story in a chapel service that had a tremendous impact on me. He told our student body, "I can still remember the temptation when I was a student here at Cincinnati Bible College. We were just out of the Depression and going through World War II, and like many college students, I had to get a part-time job to pay my way through school. I was working downtown at Pogue's Department Store in the fur department. It was my first acquaintance with furs; they fascinated me. I got to really like them, dealing with everything from fox to Persian lamb to mink to chinchilla. It was great! We cleaned them, designed them, repaired them.

"What happened was that the chief designer knew he was going to be drafted, and so they came to me and asked if I'd like to apprentice under him and take his job. They offered me $200 a week. Back in 1944, to a senior in bible college making 17 dollars and 50 cents a week preaching in a little country church, it was a fortune." After a pause, he concluded, "I quit my job at Pogue's, because I liked furs too well. I was afraid of what all that money would do to my main purpose in life of becoming a preacher."

"I quit my job . . . because I liked it too well." Please understand, Satan will try everything in his power to distract us from our main purpose of serving Christ. He'll use every temptation imaginable to entice us with what the world has to offer. He'll use every weapon in his arsenal to destroy any sense of goodness in our lives. Like Jesus Christ, we need to stand our ground. We need to allow God's goodness to echo through our lives.

NOTES

[1]Chuck Swindoll, *Sensuality: Resisting the Lure of Lust* (Portland, OR: Multnomah, 1981), p. 20.
[2]Brian Blair, "Are Churches Afraid of Cohabitation?" *The Republic* (Aug. 31, 2002).

Reflecting on Lesson Six

1. Which areas of temptation are most difficult for you to overcome? Why do you think that is?

2. Can you think of a time when you were tempted, but made the right choice? How did that make you feel?

3. Is there an area of your life that needs cleansing right now? What steps do you need to take to restore goodness?

Consider this:

How often does someone ask you to pray for them about a specific situation in their lives? How often do you actually do it? Do you tend to forget these sorts of promises as soon as you make them? If your friends were describing you, would "faithful" be an adjective they would apply to you?

7

ECHOING GOD'S FAITHFULNESS

In this lesson:

- God's faithfulness
- Spiritual faithfulness
- Standing up for your faith
- Obedience

My son Aaron and his friend Kevin signed up to work at a weekend festival in nearby Hope, Indiana, so they could earn extra credit for their high school social studies class. They got the job through the Hope Police Department. As they were picking up trash on Friday night, a couple of other teenagers who were also working wandered over their direction. These boys wore the grunge style baggy clothes and had earrings in several places besides their ears. One of them said to Aaron, "How many hours you got?"

He said, "We're doing nine."

The boy replied, "Only nine? I'm in for 32!"

I'm guessing his community service wasn't for extra credit in social studies! Why we do something is critical. God is very concerned that we serve with the right motive. The Bible says that when God's Holy Spirit lives inside of us, our behavior, our attitude, our very personality is transformed. Sometimes it happens gradually, sometimes radically, but God never leaves us the way that He finds us. We come to Him just as we are—rich or poor, clean-cut or grungy, working for extra-credit or for detention—and He immediately begins to work in us as we surrender control. His attributes echo through our lives as we mature in our Christian walk.

The Bible commands Christians to be faithful. Proverbs 3:3 says, "Let love and faithfulness never leave you; bind them around your neck, write them on the tablet of your heart." Tie faithfulness around your neck; write it on your heart. Sounds pretty important! In fact, Paul says that another key fruit of the Spirit is faithfulness. What exactly does that mean? I heard about a kamikaze pilot who volunteered for four consecutive flight missions. He was long on enthusiasm, but short on faithfulness! Faithfulness means we follow through. It implies loyalty to those we love. It is a commitment to being trustworthy. It suggests dependability, reliability, staying power.

Tie faithfulness around your neck; write it on your heart. Sounds pretty important!

Ultimately, faithfulness suggests being like God. Psalm 145:13b assures us, "The Lord is faithful to all his promises and loving toward all he has made." God always does what He says He will do. Every time we see a rainbow, it is a reminder that God is faithful to His promise: "Never again will all life be cut off by the waters of a flood." Every time we see a Bible, it is a reminder that God is faithful to His promise, "My word will never pass away." Every time we pass a church building, it is a reminder of the faithfulness of God, "I will build my church and the gates of hell will not prevail against it." Every time we take communion, it is a testimony to the faithful promise, "If we confess our sins, he is faithful and just to forgive us our sins, and cleanse us from all unrighteousness." When the trees blossom in the spring and the leaves turn to gold in the fall, it's a reminder of God's faithfulness, "As long as the earth remains, there will be seedtime and harvest, cold and heat, summer and winter, day and night." Every time we see someone respond to the invitation, it is a witness to the faithfulness of God, "My Word will not return to me empty, but will accomplish what I desire and achieve the purpose for which I sent it."

We strive to be faithful because God is faithful. The more we become like God, the more faithful we will be; the more faithful we prove to be, the more we become like God. To help us understand how to do that, we're going to once again flip through the photo album of Christ's life to catch several glimpses of what true faithfulness is all about. Faithfulness means following through with a commitment *regardless* of the difficulty. Faithfulness ultimately cost Jesus His life, but He never once violated His convictions.

The more we become like God, the more faithful we will be; the more faithful we prove to be, the more we become like God.

FAITHFUL TO GATHER FOR WORSHIP

In Luke 4:16b it says of Jesus, "On the Sabbath day he went into the synagogue, as was his custom." That's it, plain and simple. Nothing earth-shattering. No lepers healed or dead men revived, no calming a storm, walking on water, or feeding a crowd with one Happy Meal. Jesus went to the synagogue—the Jewish gathering place for worship and religious instruction and prayer—as was His custom. Apparently, He was in the habit of gathering with other believers on a weekly basis. Was that the only time He communed with God? Of course not! It may not have even been His favorite time with God. Remember, the Pharisees were largely in charge of what went on in the synagogue, and He had little patience for the arrogance and insincerity of the Pharisees. But instead of griping about all the hypocrites down at church; instead of saying, "I know a lot more about the Bible than the preacher does—I wrote it for goodness' sake!"; instead of interrupting the services every time a mistake was made; Jesus faithfully spent time every week with fellow believers.

Instead of griping about all the hypocrites down at church Jesus faithfully spent time every week with fellow believers.

A lot of people see worship as a chore to be endured, or a project to be checked off the to-do list. I once heard Tony Evans, a minister in Dallas, say that when he was a teenager, he had a drug problem. Every week his parents drug him to church! Hebrews 10:25 reminds us, "Let us not give up meeting together, as some are in the habit of doing, but let us encourage one another—and all the more as you see the Day approaching." The "Day that is approaching" refers to the return of Christ. He said we continue faithfully meeting together because it is a source of encouragement to other believers, and it keeps us focused on the promise that Christ is indeed coming back.

J. Wallace Hamilton once told of a college student who was struggling to maintain his faith but decided to go to church one Sunday anyway. During a time of prayer, he looked across the aisle two rows back and saw his biology professor with his head bowed. He concluded, "If that man, with all his intellect, can believe, so can I." He regained his faith that morning, not by what the preacher said, but by the faithfulness of one man who was simply being consistent.

Too often we allow other priorities to crowd out our faithfulness to the church. Now, I am not saying that the church is the most important thing in life, but Jesus Christ is! And when we allow our faithfulness to the church to decline, it is almost impossible for our faithfulness to Christ *not* to be affected. Jesus modeled faithfulness to corporate worship, and we need to as well. We are faithful in our attendance Monday through Friday at school and work. Why shouldn't we be faithful to worship in God's house on Sunday?

We are faithful in our attendance at school and work. Why not in God's house?

FAITHFUL TO PERSIST IN PRAYER

Luke 5:16 says, "Jesus often withdrew to lonely places and prayed." No three-year ministry was ever more hectic, more challenging, more physically and emotionally draining than Christ's ministry here on earth. The crowds constantly pressed around Him. The disciples needed regular attention and frequent correction. The opposition kept Him wary and on the move. Jesus relied on His time alone with God in prayer to sustain Him during those stressful, exhausting months of travel, teaching, and miracle-working. If the Lord of the universe needed that help, we certainly need it as well.

I once asked a professional photographer how the pros get really vivid pictures of the moon, with the landscape also well-lit. My attempts never seemed to work out right. If I exposed the picture correctly for the moon, the landscape was too dark. If I exposed the picture for the landscape, the moon became this blob of light in the sky with no definition whatsoever. He explained to me that pictures like I wanted to take are typically either perfected in the darkroom, or they involve merging two photographs into one. The camera cannot handle different lighting exposures in the same picture. In fact, he said Ansel Adams, the famous nature photographer, was really even more of a genius in the darkroom than he was with a camera in his hand.

Now, having learned that, let us suppose that I reasoned, "I don't buy it. Ansel Adams? What a rookie! He may not have been able to handle this, but I can. Professional photographers don't do it this way, but I'm up to the challenge." Well, I could say that, but it would be pretty stupid. If the best of the best know what it takes to get good pictures, I should learn from their experience.

The Son of God—Deity incarnate—God in the flesh—Jesus Christ Himself depended on prayer to sustain Him through the rigors of daily life. Why are we so apt to ignore our own need for the same help? Why do you think prayer was fine for Jesus, but it is not necessary for you? Why do I strive to be so faithful when it comes to sermon preparation, but then I'm often so unfaithful when it comes to praying over the sermon I have pre-

The Son of God—Deity incarnate—depended on prayer to sustain Him.

pared? Colossians 4:2 insists, "Devote yourselves to prayer, being watchful and thankful." Devote yourselves to prayer. Jesus certainly did, and if He needed it, we need it even more. If He wanted it to be a central focus of His life, then we would be wise to maintain the same focus.

FAITHFUL TO MAINTAIN HEALTHY RELATIONSHIPS

In John chapter 15, Jesus talks to His disciples about His upcoming death, their grief that would turn to joy, and the promise of the Holy Spirit. He said to them in verses 15b-16, "I have called you friends, for everything that I learned from my Father I have made known to you. You did not choose me, but I chose you and appointed you to go and bear fruit—fruit that will last." We see a consistent pattern with Jesus in the Gospels. He was faithful to His disciples. It is true that He confronted them at times. He often had to reprimand them for things like selfishness, anger, jealousy, and unbelief. Through it all, He loved them deeply; He always kept their best interest in mind. He rejoiced over their victories and celebrated their accomplishments. He even served them, despite the fact that He had every right to demand that they serve Him.

Faithfulness, what we might refer to as loyalty or devotion, is essential to strong and healthy relationships. I have a pillow on a chair in my office that says, *"A friend knows all about you. . . . And still likes you!"* We all need friends like that. We also need to be friends like that! Romans 12:9-10 tells us, "Love must be sincere. Hate what is evil; cling to what is good. Be devoted to one another in brotherly love. Honor one another above yourselves." What kind of friend are you? Are you always the one asking for help, or do you offer help as well? Are you quick to point out a mistake or eager to offer a compliment? Do you find yourself joining in the latest gossip, or do you come to the defense of the person who is being maligned? Do you abandon your friends when the going gets tough, or do you hang in there when life isn't fun and they are depressing to be around?

Let's bring it home: Are you faithful in your relationship to your mate? Ephesians 5:33 says to husbands, "Each one of you also must love his wife as he loves himself, and the wife must respect her husband." How about it? Are you loving at home? Respectful? Faithful in mind and heart as well as in body? When couples get married, they repeat marriage vows which state: "For better, for worse; for richer, for poorer; in sickness and in health." One groom thought it was multiple choice and said, "I'll take better, richer, and healthy!" That is not how it works! Couples do not say, "I'm going to *try* to love you for better, for worse; for richer, for poorer; in sickness and in health." You did not say, "I *hope* to honor and cherish you." I did not say, "Gail, I'll *give it my best shot* to be faithful to you, so long as we both shall live." We say, "I *promise* to love you; I *promise* to honor you; I *promise* to cherish you; I *promise* to be faithful to you." Unless your spouse violates that marriage covenant through adultery or abandonment or violent abuse, you are expected to keep your promise, and so am I. It is part of being faithful.

The September 2002 *Focus on the Family Newsletter* contained data from the National Survey of Family and Households conducted by a research team which studied 5232 married adults in the late 1980s. Of those adults, 645 reported being *unhappily* married. Five years later, those same adults—some of whom had divorced or separated and others who had remained married—were interviewed again. The results were startling. Two-thirds of the unhappily married spouses who stayed married were happier five years later. Of those who initially rated their marriages as *"very unhappy,"* but remained together, nearly 80% considered themselves *"happily married"* five years later. On the other hand, only 19% of those who got divorced or separated were happy five years later. There is something to be said for staying faithful!

Are things not going so well for you at home right now? Hang in there. Echo God's faithfulness. I cannot promise it will get better because it takes two to nurture a fulfilling marriage. But please don't bail out. The presence of God's Holy Spirit inside of you can help you endure the struggle. If it is too late for you, if your marriage has already crumbled, God can help you heal from the hurt, and He will enable you to put your life back together and move on. But please be very cautious about repeating those vows a second or third time. Faithfulness does not get easier just because the scenery changes. We all have to work like crazy to honor the vows we make before God. Being faithful in relationships is part of being a Spirit-filled Christian.

Hang in there. Echo God's faithfulness.

The mother of a friend recently died at 80 years of age. Many years ago, she wrote a personal mission statement for her life that she strove every day to live out. It contained a list of goals such as: to start each day with prayer; to have compassion for all people; to be an encourager; to be gracious in receiving either gifts or compliments; to treat with dignity everyone with whom I come in contact; to be a peacemaker; to thoughtfully listen, but only give counsel when asked; to be a helpful neighbor; to be willing to do that which is requested even if I have to stretch my talents; to do my part in keeping the ties within my family loving and secure. You know what that is? It is called being faithful in relationships. It is what Jesus did, and what we need to do too.

FAITHFUL TO STAND FIRM IN THE TRUTH

Seventy-eight times in the New Testament Jesus said, "I tell you the truth." The King James Version translates this as "Verily, verily, I say unto you. . . ." Jesus was always faithful to the truth. He told it, He taught it, and He lived it. In much the same way, being faithful to stand firm in the truth suggests a variety of things for us. It includes being honest in the words we say. It means we stand up for truth when others deny it. It means we do what we say we are going to do. We keep our word. Chuck Swindoll said at a Promise-Keepers rally several years ago, "It's not Promise-Makers, it's Promise-Keepers!" Faithful Christians do not just tell the truth; they live the truth.

Faithful Christians do not just tell the truth; they live the truth.

For instance, faithful Christians fulfill their responsibilities at church. At our church, like yours, we have those men and women and young people who consistently work in the nursery and drive the church van and serve as care shepherds and provide assistance in numerous other behind-the-scenes capacities. They don't get a lot of glory, but we could not get along without them.

Following through once our initial enthusiasm starts to wane is not always easy, but finishing what we start is a matter of faithfulness. Faithful Christians pay their bills. We agreed to certain terms when we signed the lease, or took out that loan, or bought that new furniture. As strict as our budget has to be, we need to hold up our end of the bargain. Faithful Christians remain generous to God. It is challenging at times to be consistent in our giving. We don't know how we can meet all our obligations if we give ten percent of our income to Christ's church. But the Lord promises to bless those who are generous. And God is faithful too. He will see that we are cared for. Faithful Christians stand up for godly values in an increasingly immoral culture. Your kids may push those boundaries to the limit, your coworkers may criticize your puritanical views, you may find yourself opposed at every turn. But faithfulness means we stand firm in the truth. Notice what it says in Psalm 15:1-2,4b, "Lord, who may dwell in your sanctuary? Who may live on your holy hill? He whose walk is blameless and who does what is righteous, who speaks the truth from his heart . . . who keeps his oath even when it hurts."

Erika Harold of Illinois was crowned Miss America 2003. According to the *Pastor's Weekly Briefing* from Focus on the Family, her official platform for the Miss Illinois phase of the competition was abstinence education, despite critics who warned her not to take such an "unpopular" issue to the national level. In fact, State pageant officials changed her Miss America platform to "teen violence prevention," calling it more "pertinent." However, Miss Harold, who is also a dedicated Christian, reported that she had been ordered by pageant officials to stop talking publicly about sexual abstinence, something she has advocated for years to over 14,000 teenagers in Illinois. To her credit, she insisted at a news conference the following Tuesday, "I will not be bullied." Sandy Rios, President of *Concerned Women for America* said, "This is blatant censorship. . . . They are attacking Erika Harold's values. . . . In an age when beauty queens are regularly disqualified for inappropriate behavior, who would have thought that a virtuous one would be silenced for her virtue." The next day, pageant officials reversed themselves and agreed to let Harold speak about sexual-abstinence education.[1] Her faithfulness to stand for truth should serve as a reminder to us as well.

FAITHFUL TO DO GOD'S WILL

Following His Last Supper with the Disciples, and just before the crucifixion, Luke 22:39-43 says,

> Jesus went out as usual to the Mount of Olives, and his disciples followed him. On reaching the place, he said to them, "Pray that you will not fall into temptation." He withdrew about a stone's throw beyond them, knelt down and prayed, "Father, if you are willing, take this cup from me; yet not my will, but yours be done." An angel from heaven appeared to him and strengthened him.

In the books, and now the blockbuster movies *The Lord of the Rings*, J.R.R. Tolkien weaves a tale of suspense, wonder, and the relentless struggle of good versus evil. His trilogy has remained unparalleled in contemporary literature. The prequel to those novels is *The Hobbit*, a fantasy story about dwarves and elves and dragons and wizards, and little people called hobbits. As the story progresses, a hobbit by the name of Bilbo Baggins is hired by a group of dwarves to regain some of their stolen treasure from a dangerous dragon. Bilbo did not want to do it. He was terrified at the thought of it, but he had promised to do it, so he did.

As he crept down the tunnel that led to the dragon's lair, he could see the glow of the dragon's orange skin; he could smell the sulfur of his vaporous breath; he could hear the heavy breathing as the dragon slept. Bilbo was overcome with terror at what he was about to face. Should he proceed, or should he retreat? Tolkien wrote, "It was at this point that Bilbo stopped. Going on from there was the bravest thing he ever did. The tremendous things that happened afterward were as nothing compared to it. He fought the real battle in the tunnel alone, before he ever saw the vast danger that lay in wait."[2] The real battle was with himself, and his own dread. Once he resolved those fears and pressed on, the battle was essentially won.

> The real battle was with himself, and his own dread.

When I read that description of Bilbo's inner turmoil, I thought immediately of Christ's experience in the Garden of Gethsemane on the night before His death. I am not trying to diminish the significance of Christ's struggle in the Garden by using Tolkien's fantasy story as an example, but the parallels are striking. Jesus had come to the Garden of Gethsemane for a final time of prayer before His final suffering and anguish began. He was nearly overwhelmed by dread. This was His hour of struggle. This was His moment of hesitancy. Matthew quotes Jesus, "My soul is overwhelmed with sorrow to the point of death. . . ." Mark said of Him, "He was deeply distressed and troubled. . . ." Luke recorded that, "Jesus, being in anguish, prayed more earnestly, and His sweat was like drops of blood falling to the ground." His next steps were decisive and confident, even in the face of tremendous pain, but in this moment He wavered.

Don't let it bother you that He longed for a way out. The fact that He was hesitant proves He was human. The fact that He followed through proves He was more than a human being. A paraphrase of Tolkien's words describes well the conflict within Christ at this moment. "He fought the real battle in the garden alone, before He ever faced the vast danger that lay in wait." "Going on from there was the bravest thing He ever did." An intense struggle took place the night before Jesus' death that we seldom comprehend. Our Lord dreaded the cross, not because He was afraid to die, but because of what His death would involve. He was about to bear the sin and guilt of the whole world. All other ago-

> You can call it duty, commitment, sacrifice, or love, but there's no question that Jesus was faithful to His mission.

nies ever experienced would pale in comparison to the anguish Jesus was about to endure. He longed to be home with the Father, safe in His arms, once again recognized as Lord of Heaven and Earth. But He had a job to do. He had a world to save. So you can call it duty, commitment, sacrifice, love. But there's no question that Jesus was faithful to His mission.

How about us? We will never be asked to bear the sins of the world, but we are expected to carry out God's will. In Matthew 25:23 Jesus concluded one of His parables, "The master replied, 'Well done, good and faithful servant! You have been faithful with a few things; I will put you in charge of many things. Come and share your master's happiness!'" We need to faithfully carry out God's will, even when it is hard. That is our duty as Christians. We often hear of teachers, youth workers, church leaders, or ministers who say they are burned out on ministry. One father commented, "The fourth-grade Sunday School teacher quit because of burnout. I have a feeling my son was the arsonist!" I understand that workers can get burned out after a long period of constant service. We all need time away to get refreshed and rejuvenated, but we can't let burnout become an excuse for misplaced priorities. Faithfulness means obeying God, doing His will, following through on His plan. We are called to be faithful when we are busy as well as when we have nothing to do, in bad times as well as good times, in sickness and in health, in boredom as well as excitement, in little things as well as big things. Faithfulness means obeying God.

Stuart Briscoe and his wife Jill came to the United States from England years ago, and he now preaches at the Elmbrook Church in Wisconsin. I once heard Stuart share about the time in his life shortly after he graduated from high school when he had decided to join the Royal Marines. A friend of the family was a Captain in the Royal Marines as well as a strong Christian. He came to see Stuart shortly before he left for basic training. He said, "Stuart, you will, of course, nail your colors to the mast."

Faithfulness means obeying God.

Stuart responded, "What does that mean?" The captain explained that years ago, when British warships sailed into battle, they flew the flag, the colors, of Great Britain. If things went badly in battle, the flag could be lowered, and a white flag would be flown to signify surrender. Occasionally, in the thick of battle, a captain would send someone up the mast to nail the flag's rope directly to the mast. By doing this, the colors could not be lowered; he would be saying, in effect, "We fight to the death. No surrender."

The older man again said, "Stuart, you will, of course, nail your colors to the mast! There is no surrender!"

Jesus Christ is the Lord of our lives. Living for Him is a 24/7 proposition. We nail our colors to the mast. We live for Him no matter the consequences. We echo His faithfulness despite the pressure to cave in to the influences of our culture. There is no surrender.

NOTES

[1] *Pastor's Weekly Briefing* (Colorado Springs: Focus on the Family, Oct. 11, 2002).

[2] J.R.R. Tolkien, *The Hobbit* (New York: Ballantine Books, a division of Random House, 1966), p. 205.

Reflecting on Lesson Seven

1. Can you think of a time when someone broke faith with you? How did that make you feel?

2. Have you ever stood your ground on something, only to be opposed or even attacked? What happened? Should you have handled things differently?

3. What is one area of your life where you need to step up in this matter of faithfulness? What can you do this week to practice this vital quality?

Consider this:

It is one o'clock in the morning. Your teenage daughter has come home from a date. She comes into your room crying and says, "Daddy, I think I'm pregnant." How would you react/respond to this situation?

8

ECHOING GOD'S GENTLENESS

In this lesson:

- Being approachable
- Separating gentleness from weakness
- Showing compassion

I went through the drive-through window at an Arby's Restaurant down south some time ago, and as I pulled out of the parking lot, I noticed a sign that said: "Do you have a great smile? Great attitude? We're hiring you!" Notice, they didn't ask, "Do you know roast beef? Can you broil chicken? Have you ever curled a French fry before?" They were more interested in personality than ability. In much the same way, Jim Parker, CEO of

Southwest Airlines, reported that their company's hiring process involves at least a half dozen interviews. However, they do not include aptitude testing. He explained, "We don't care much about education and experience, because we can train people to do whatever they have to do. We look for listening, caring, smiling, warm people. We hire *attitudes*."

We're nearing the end of the Fruit of the Spirit list: "Love, joy, peace, patience, kindness, goodness, faithfulness, gentleness and self-control." So far, we have seen seven key characteristics that originate with God and then should echo through our lives as we seek to become more like Christ and do our best to impact others around us. These remaining two traits should also reverberate through our lives as we surrender to the power of God's Holy Spirit.

The fruit of the Spirit is gentleness, and yet the world is not a very gentle place. Remember the snipers in Washington D.C.? We wonder how anyone could indiscriminately aim an assault rifle at a person he has never even met and pull the trigger—it is incomprehensible. We face the ongoing threat of terrorism from the al-Qaeda network and other extremist groups. In the town where I preach, the number of battered women who need the services of our local shelter has increased dramatically. We see an overwhelming lack of gentleness in today's culture. The world is not a gentle place because gentleness is not a human quality. Certain individuals may naturally be more calm or sensitive than others, but because our sinful nature is predisposed to selfishness, true gentleness only comes as a by-product of God's Spirit living within us. It truly is a *fruit* of the Spirit.

The world is not a very gentle place.

Do you remember the old television show *Gentle Ben*? A little boy had a pet bear—big, strong, potentially dangerous—but gentle. That is the image I want you to consider in this chapter. Gentleness is *not* a synonym for frailty or helplessness. Rather, like the trait of meekness, gentleness suggests strength under control. It is the intentional decision to submit our will to the will of God; to allow His tenderness and compassion to shine through our lives. And the fact is, no one has ever echoed this godly trait better than Jesus. He was no pushover: The morning He cleared the temple of those who were buying and selling, He proved He could handle corruption. The day He pronounced the seven woes on the hypocritical religious leaders, He demonstrated His intolerance for evil. The afternoon He died on the cross, He showed the strength of character to give His life for the sins of the world. Jesus was tough as nails, there is no doubt about that. Yet, someone has said, "The Almighty did not act 'High and mighty.' The only One who was holy did not act 'Holier than thou.' The only One who knew it all did not act like a 'Know-it-all.' And the One who owns all the stuff never 'Strutted His stuff.'" Jesus maintained His firmness and strength of character without exhibiting arrogance or aggression.

Gentleness is *not* a synonym for frailty or helplessness.

Matthew 11:29 describes Jesus as "gentle and humble in heart." Second Corinthians 10:1 refers to the "meekness and gentleness of Christ." Even when He walked this earth as a man, all authority belonged to Him; He had unlimited power and unparalleled strength. Still, He could gently touch the shoulder of a leper and bring cleansing. He could tenderly wipe away the tear of an adulteress and restore her dignity. He could softly whisper a word to the lifeless body of a little girl and renew life. Gentle Jesus, our "Gentle Shepherd." Despite His awesome power, He maintained a tender touch. Perhaps no story better communicates the gentleness of our Lord than His interaction with children, so let's consider that incident in His life to discover how to better echo this quality through our own lives.

Mark 10:13-16 relates,

> People were bringing little children to Jesus to have him touch them, but the disciples rebuked them. When Jesus saw this, he was indignant. He said to them, "Let the little children come to me, and do not hinder them, for the kingdom of God belongs to such as these. I tell you the truth, anyone who will not receive the kingdom of God like a little child will never enter it." And he took the children in his arms, put his hands on them and blessed them.

GENTLENESS SUGGESTS THAT WE ARE APPROACHABLE

It has been said, "Tact is the ability to make people feel at home when you wish that they were!" Jesus had that ability. People felt comfortable bringing their children to Him. They wanted Him to bestow a blessing—to give them some ray of hope about the future. And He took the time to welcome each child, to encourage each child, to interact with each child individually.

Do you ever find yourself overlooking people? Our worship minister asked me to give a brief devotion at a meeting one night at church. I was running a little late. When I got there, I was reading over my notes, so I said hello to a few people, but I failed to walk across the room and talk to several men who were already there when I came in. It wasn't a big thing, and I am sure none of them lost any sleep over it. But as I was driving off to my next appointment, I was kicking myself for once again being so preoccupied. I blew the chance to talk to some men who were working really hard to make our Christmas program a success. I can be bad about that sometimes, so focused on one thing that I miss those who are right in front of me. Do you ever do that?

Jesus knew how downtrodden the people of Palestine were, how badly they needed some encouragement, so He was approachable. On one occasion, when He was on His way to Jairus's house to heal his daughter, a sick woman touched the hem of His cloak for a healing of her own. Rather than resenting the interruption, Jesus took the time to affirm and encourage her. Still another time, Jesus sailed across the Sea of Galilee with His disciples for some much-needed solitude and rest, but the crowds met Him upon His arrival. Rather than sending them away, He taught them. And here we find Him stopped by several anxious parents. Times were hard, food was scarce, the political scene was often tense. Would Jesus take a moment to bless the little children being raised under such uncertain conditions? His response: "Let the little children come to Me!"

How did they know He would do that? Because Jesus was the kind of person who cared for children. I imagine He smiled at kids a lot. He got down on the floor and played with them, and He always laughed at their silly jokes. He often gave the most attention to those whom others thought were insignificant.

Several years ago, Robert Ringer wrote a national bestseller entitled, *Winning through Intimidation.* That is the approach many people take. Put the other person on the defensive, never lower your guard, maintain a competitive edge, and, above all, intimidate the competition. Jesus did not win through intimidation, He won through compassion. His gentleness was evident because He was approachable.

His gentleness was evident because He was approachable.

We need to do that, to build bridges instead of walls. That involves things like listening carefully before speaking. If every time you open up to your friend, he or she criticizes what you have to say, or always interrupts you before you get to the main point, it won't be long before you just stop opening up. Or how many times do we, as parents, do this to our kids? They approach us about a problem, and instead of listening to how they really feel, we immediately point out why the problem is their fault, or we offer some quick-fix solution, when all they really want is to be heard and understood. After a while, they may simply stop talking to us. When faced with a tough issue, some of us immediately try to explain away the problem or defend ourselves before listening to what the person is really trying to say. In a discussion, instead of hearing what the other person needs to communicate, all the time that they're talking, we're trying to think of a good response. Gentleness means we're approachable. Being approachable means we listen.

It also means we refuse to overreact when others disappoint us. Shortly after I got my driver's license, I was meeting my parents at a mall for supper. As I pulled into the parking space, I somehow managed to hit the gas pedal instead of the brake and ran into a parked car. Following the initial sound of impact, a piece of the other car's grill fell out onto the pavement with a hollow, clanking sound. I can still hear it to this very day. It was one of the more sickening sounds I had ever heard. I went into the mall to find my folks. As soon as they saw my ashen face, they said, "Mark, what's wrong?" I told them I had had a wreck, and the first words out of their mouth were, "Are you all right?" They didn't ask, "How's the car?" but "Are you all right?" Now, in all honesty, I was driving a tank disguised as a station wagon, so there was not much reason for them to ask about the car, but it is nice that they

Being approachable means we listen.

didn't. My parents nearly always maintained a spirit of gentleness through potentially volatile situations, so I was comfortable talking with them about almost anything. Parents, if we are gentle, our sons are not afraid to ask us tough questions. Our daughters will not hesitate to talk over tough issues. They may have a problem, they may be in trouble, they may know we will be hurt and disappointed, but they should also know we will not go ballistic on them. We will not disown or disinherit them.

An employee should have the confidence to talk over a problem with the boss knowing he will not lose his temper. A supervisor should be able to address an issue with an employee without worrying that he will overreact or take it too personally. A neighbor should be able to make a suggestion without your flying off the handle. A Bible school teacher should be able to discuss a discipline problem concerning your child without your becoming defensive. Gentleness means we don't overreact.

Building bridges means we put others' needs before our own. When it is time for dessert, you do not have to lunge for the biggest piece of pie. When your wife is not feeling well, you can pitch in and help out around the house. When bad news comes, you do not just think about how it will impact you, you think about the impact it will have on those around you. When cutbacks at work threaten your job, you do not just think about your own security, but you are sensitive to those who are facing similar pressure.

Gentleness means we don't overreact.

John Gunther, in his book *Death Be Not Proud,* told of the death of his 18-year-old son, Johnny. Johnny was handsome, popular, and an excellent student. He passed the entrance exams to Columbia University two weeks before he died of a brain tumor. Following his initial operation, when the seriousness of the situation was first discovered, the surgeon asked Johnny's parents about the advisability of telling him the full gravity of the situation. They decided that he was so intelligent, he would probably suspect anyway, so they thought it best to explain everything. The surgeon went into Johnny's hospital room alone. In a matter-of-fact tone of voice, he laid out to the young man the reality of the situation. The prognosis did not look good. Johnny listened carefully, and then looked the doctor in the eye and asked, "How should we break the news to my parents?"

Gentleness means we are approachable. One way we cultivate this quality is to think of other's needs before our own. Jesus welcomed these little children, in spite of the fact that He had troubles of His own. You see, He was on His way to Jerusalem knowing that the cross awaited Him. At that moment, He had many other worries to consider besides these children. And yet, there they were, standing in line, waiting to be blessed. How could He ignore them?

The disciples recognized the great stress Jesus was under, so they attempted to disperse the crowd. They tried to keep the children from bothering their Master. But read again Jesus' reaction in verses 14-15, "When Jesus saw this, he was indignant. He said to them, 'Let the little children come to me, and do not hinder them, for the kingdom of God belongs to such as these. I tell you the truth, anyone who will not receive the kingdom of God like a little child will never enter it.'" He confronted the disciples, clarifying the value and significance of children.

GENTLENESS DOES NOT INDICATE THAT WE ARE WEAK

We do not usually think of gentleness as a compliment. A friend told me about a new support group called the D.O.O.R.M.A.T.S.

That is an acrostic for, "Dependent Order Of Really Meek And Timid Souls." Their motto is, *"The meek shall inherit the earth . . . if that's okay with everybody."* That is often the impression we have of those who are gentle: doormats. However, gentleness has nothing to do with weakness or cowardice. Abraham Lincoln was once described as, "Velvet Steel." He was tough. He was firm. But he was also gentle. As was Jesus. You see, as friendly as He was with the children, He was just that firm with His own disciples. He communicated His frustration with them in a very forthright way. Mark says He became indignant. He put His foot down and demanded: "Let the children come to me and do not hinder them."

Abraham Lincoln was once described as "Velvet Steel."

The disciples meant well. They were concerned about Jesus. They had taken the responsibility of His well-being upon themselves. They did not want Him to overdo it. They knew if He gave an inch, the crowds would take a mile. And they knew that Jesus was such a caring person, He would not turn anybody away. However, Jesus realized they had failed to take into consideration the needs of the children and their parents. He had come to meet people at their point of need, not avoid people to meet His own needs. By His tone of voice and the look on His face, the disciples immediately realized they had overstepped their bounds. Jesus became frustrated by their misguided attempt to protect Him. Therefore, once He got their attention, He corrected their misunderstanding. "The Kingdom of God belongs to children. They are models for adults to follow—so trusting, so eager, so loving, so pure. If adults don't receive the kingdom like a child would, they'll never enter in."

I want you to understand what was happening here: Jesus was not acting like some politician kissing babies just to win the votes of moms and dads. He was prioritizing these kids. He said they were dramatically important, not because of the parents they belonged to, but because of who they were. In this text, Jesus was forced to confront the attitude of His best friends because they misunderstood the value of individuals, and the impact He was seeking to make.

When we find ourselves in confrontational situations as Jesus did, we need to be both gentle and firm—Velvet Steel. Gentleness balances strength with sensitivity. It means we refuse to condemn. A recent Harvard graduate was traveling down in Kentucky when he stopped at a gas station to fill up his Jaguar. The attendant could tell by the man's accent that he was from out of town, so—trying to be friendly—he asked, "Hey, Buddy, where you from?"

Looking down his nose at the employee, the man said, "I will tell you this: I come from a place where no one ends a sentence with a preposition."

"Oh. Well, where are you from . . . Jerk?!"

Neither of the participants in this conversation displayed gentleness. That's how disagreements escalate into feuds!

I consider Jesus' confrontation with the disciples further evidence of His gentleness because He took the time to explain why they were wrong. His response was logical and controlled. I wonder how people in our culture perceive Christians. Are we gentle when it comes to confrontation, or are we abrasive? Are we considerate or abusive? Do we respect who they are, even if we do not respect what they stand for, or do we attack their character and slander their opinions? This applies to dramatic issues like opposition to abortion and gay-rights legislation. If we come across as mean-spirited and

> We may win an argument and lose the people.

hateful, we may win an argument, but we will have little chance of winning any people. But it also applies to daily inconveniences. How do we respond if somebody cuts in front of us at the checkout line? Or, heaven forbid, they bring eleven items into the "Ten Items or Less" express lane? Confession time: Have you ever counted the number of items in the person's cart in front of you? I have! How do you deal with the auto mechanic who says the car will be ready at 4:30, but you end up waiting for it until 5:45? How about the store employee who says, "No problem" over the phone, but then says, "I'm sorry, we can't do that," once you've driven to the store. Now remember, gentleness sometimes requires that we be firm. God did not command us to be doormats. But He did say that if the Holy Spirit lives in our lives, we will learn to deal gently with people, even those who give us grief or cause us trouble.

When we do have to be firm, we should always confront with the purpose of restoration. Jesus corrected His disciples because He wanted them to better understand His purpose and mission, and He hoped they would handle things differently the next time. Second Timothy 2:24-26 reminds us,

> The Lord's servant must not quarrel; instead, he must be kind to everyone, able to teach, not resentful. Those who oppose him he must *gently instruct,* in the hope that God will grant them repentance leading them to a knowledge of the truth, and that they will come to their senses and escape from the trap of the devil, who has taken them captive to do his will.

Confrontation, even if it has to be firm, can still be handled gently. Rather than exhibiting a critical spirit and a sour disposition, and then coming off with a vengeful response, we need to choose our

Confrontation, even if it has to be firm, can still be handled gently.

words carefully, and make sure our goal is to help the situation improve, to help the other person improve. That brings us to the final aspect of gentleness that Jesus modeled in this text.

GENTLENESS DEMANDS THAT WE SHOW COMPASSION

Mark 10:16 says, "He took the children in his arms, put his hands on them and blessed them." Notice, Jesus gave them His undivided attention. Looking them in the eye, and using appropriate, loving touch, He made sure these kids knew that in that moment, they were the only thing on His mind. Paul Harvey said that he and his wife were listening to a sermon one day in which the minister was talking about the importance of communicating love through touching. The preacher remarked, "It's a proven fact that little babies who are touched and held gain weight 30% faster than babies that are left alone." Mrs. Harvey leaned over and said, "Don't you ever touch me again!"

It is amazing how most children respond to positive touch. When my son Daniel was little, he had a burr haircut. Every time he walked past me, it was impossible not to rub his head! And I wasn't the only one. Other people did it too. All the time! And you know what? I think he liked it! Jesus recognized that both children and adults need loving contact in daily doses. An arm around the shoulder, a hug, even a high-five can help us express focused attention through touch. It is a compassionate response to others' need for affirmation. It is a mark of gentleness and sensitivity.

> Jesus affirmed the tremendous value of children.

And did you notice that Jesus affirmed the tremendous value of these kids as well? He took them in His arms, He put His hands on them, and *He blessed them.* What do you suppose He might have said? God told Moses in Numbers chapter 6 how the Old Testament priests were to bless people: "The Lord bless you and keep you; the Lord make His face shine upon you, and be gracious to you; the Lord turn His face toward you and give you peace." Jesus might have said that, but I tend to think He was more personal. Remember, He could look into each child's eyes, and know what his or her future would hold. He might have said, "Joshua, you will be a gifted teacher someday. Study hard and use your gifts to change lives. Sarah, you possess a strong and determined spirit. Stand firm against the evils of our time. Nathaniel, you will be a man of great influence. Lead your people wisely." To each one, Jesus spoke words of encouragement and affirmation. He challenged them to be godly, and He instructed them to be strong. Proverbs 16:24 says, "Pleasant words are a honeycomb, sweet to the soul and healing to the bones."

Now, these weren't empty words from Jesus just to boost self-esteem. *Time* Magazine printed a very interesting essay recently entitled, "Lacking in Self-Esteem? Good for You!" The author, Andrew Sullivan, pointed out that many children have been educated in recent years according to the theory that if they lack self-esteem, they will have trouble making it in this world. We have been told that the worst thing we could ever do to a child is to tell him he is not "all that." Sullivan wrote, "New research has found that self-esteem can be just as high among D students, drunk drivers and former Presidents from Arkansas as it is among Nobel laureates, nuns and New York City fire fighters." He continued, "Racists, street thugs, and school bullies all polled high on the self-esteem charts. And you can see why. If you think you're God's gift, you're particularly offended if other people don't treat you that way." Still further, he said, when it comes to education, "When the kids have been told from Day One that they can do no

When children are told they can do no wrong, they can develop the wrong kind of self-worth.

wrong, when every grade in high school is assessed so as to make the kid feel good rather than to give an accurate measure of his work, the student can develop self-worth dangerously unrelated to the objective truth."[1]

Jesus was not offering phony self-esteem building with no basis in reality. He blessed these children to encourage them, to challenge them, and to guide them. He did it because He was gentle, compassionate, and aware of their needs. Colossians 4:6 adds, "Let your conversation be always full of grace, seasoned with salt, so that you may know how to answer everyone." The fruit of the Spirit is gentleness.

A preacher friend told me about Tammy Trent, a Christian singer that he heard share her testimony, her faith story. She and her husband were in Jamaica when he went scuba diving. Something went horribly wrong, and he drowned. His death occurred just before September 11th of 2001, so Tammy was unable to get home. Likewise, her friends and family were unable to get to her. Stranded there all alone, she sat in her hotel room sobbing over her loss. She just kept praying, "Lord, I can't get through this. I need you to send me an angel, just one angel to wrap his arms around me and hold me. Please God. . . ."

Tammy said later, "Suddenly, I heard a knock on the door, and there was my angel. Granted, she was dressed in the uniform of a Hilton cleaning woman, but I knew God had sent her to me. Seeing my face, she asked, 'Are you all right?' I fought back tears and said, 'No.' She said, 'You're grieving, aren't you.' Then she put her cleaning supplies down and took me in her arms as I sobbed on her shoulder. She asked, 'Are you a Christian? Can I pray with you?' Then, this cleaning woman prayed the most comforting prayer I've ever heard. Finally, when I had regained my composure, I sat reading my Bible while she cleaned the room; and as she cleaned, she sang hymns and praise choruses, one after another. I prayed for God to come, and He came through her." The fruit of the Spirit is gentleness. It means we treat people with the sensitivity, the compassion, the tenderness of Christ Himself. We echo the gentleness of God.

> Gentleness means we treat people with the sensitivity and the tenderness of Christ Himself.

NOTES

[1]Andrew Sullivan, "Lacking in Self-Esteem? Good for You!" *Time* (Oct. 14, 2002): 102.

Reflecting on Lesson Eight

1. Can you think of a character from history, or literature, or even the movies who exudes a personality of "velvet steel"? How does this person model both strength and tenderness?

2. Do you find that gentleness comes naturally for you, or is it a struggle? How would you back up your answer?

3. What is an area of your life that would benefit from exercising gentleness? What could you do to implement it this week?

Consider this:

Many people today seem full of anger and ready to answer every situation with violence. Do you ever find your own emotions so out of control that you say or do things you wish you hadn't? What was the fallout from your lack of control? What is your excuse for such behavior? What, if anything, have you done to change your behavior?

9 ECHOING GOD'S SELF-CONTROL

In this lesson:

- The destructiveness of lack of control
- The definition of self-control
- The importance of self-control
- Jesus' example
- Advice to consider when losing control

On Friday night, December 9, 1977, life changed forever for professional basketball players Rudy Tomjanovich of the Houston Rockets, and Kermit Washington of the Los Angeles Lakers. When a fight broke out between Washington and Kevin Kunnert of Houston, Tomjanovich ran toward center court to help break up the fight. Sensing Tomjanovich's approach, Washington spun around and threw a vicious right hook that shattered Rudy's face. It took five surgeries to repair the damage, but it took A.A. and faith to help Rudy Tomjanovich overcome the drinking problem and the nightmares that came in the years following the attack.

For Kermit Washington, a few stitches repaired his damaged fist, but the years have not taken away the pain of that night. The threats, rejection, and stereotypes of violence persisted long after the fight itself. A failed business, a failed marriage, and a failed radio career still haunt him today. He attributes his inability to get a coaching job at any level to the shock waves of the punch he threw decades ago. Both men have expressed regret over the events of that night. Each wishes the other well in the years to come. A $2 million settlement was enforced to help make things right. Following that fateful punch, the NBA instituted far stiffer penalties for on-court violence. But the bottom line is that all those years of heartache and pain were the result of one brief moment of a loss of control. *Sports Illustrated* ran this story on the 25th anniversary of the fight, but the *New York Times* may have said it best when they featured an article in May of 2000, "A Sudden, Violent Moment That Still Haunts a Life."[1]

The Apostle Paul tells us that the Fruit of the Spirit, the product of God's Holy Spirit living inside of us as Christians, is self-control. Consider our theme text one final time, Galatians 5:22-23, "The fruit of the Spirit is love, joy, peace, patience, kindness, goodness, faithfulness, gentleness and self-control. Against such things there is no law." Against such things there is no law. Nobody makes laws against traits like these. No laws are necessary when these attributes rule in our hearts.

Three chapters back, we dealt with the characteristic of goodness. We looked at Jesus' example in the wilderness when Satan tempted Him to gratify fleshly desires, satisfy materialistic desires, and fulfill ego desires. We summarized those temptations as lust, greed, and pride. In each case, Jesus was good. He was pure. He did the right thing. Now that we have come to self-control, the question arises, "How is this different from goodness?" For our purposes here, because goodness dealt with our outward actions, we will consider self-control from the perspective of our emotions. The failure to keep our inner selves—our emotions—under control frequently leads to the loss of control in other areas of life. The fruit of the Spirit is self-control. What does that mean?

The failure to keep our inner selves under control frequently leads to the loss of control in other areas of life.

THE DEFINITION OF SELF-CONTROL

Self-control does not simply mean we control ourselves. Are you familiar with the term oxymoron? An oxymoron is a single phrase made up of seemingly contradictory terms. Examples include jumbo shrimp, rubber cement, peaceful confrontation, Hell's Angels, military intelligence, and short sermon! In many ways, self-control is an oxymoron; those two things do not go together. The Greek philosopher Epictetus said, "No man is free who is not master of himself." That is not entirely true. No matter how hard we try, we cannot master ourselves.

James stated in his epistle that the tongue is a restless evil, full of deadly poison. We cannot control it. The Apostle Paul wrote in Romans 7:21-23,

> So I find this law at work: When I want to do good, evil is

> right there with me. For in my inner being I delight in God's law; but I see another law at work in the members of my body, waging war against the law of my mind and making me a prisoner of the law of sin.

Paul says we cannot control our minds. A war is going on in there! First Thessalonians 4:4 speaks of "the heathens who cannot control their own bodies, but pursue passionate lusts." Romans 8:8 summarizes, "Those controlled by the sinful nature cannot please God." It is impossible! These verses demonstrate man's inability to master his own body and his various passions.

However, just because we cannot control ourselves, that is not an excuse for living life out of control. I once saw a cartoon of a boy who is showing his dad his report card. His dad asks, "How do you explain these awful grades?" The son replies, "I don't know, Dad. Do you think we should blame heredity or environment?" Our culture promotes such a victim mentality today: "It's not my fault." "I'm not responsible for my actions." "My parents are to blame." "The culture corrupted me!" The truth is, we may not be able to control ourselves, but we can allow God to control us. Epictetus should have said, "No man is free who does not have God as his master."

We may not be able to control ourselves, but we can allow God to control us.

Regarding this Fruit of the Spirit, Rick Warren explained in one of his sermons that "Self-control doesn't mean Self-*IN*-Control: It means, Self-*UNDER*-Control." It suggests we are under the control of God. My whole person, your whole being—body, soul and spirit—we are completely subject to the sovereignty of God. First Corinthians 6:19-20 explains,

> Do you not know that your body is a temple of the Holy Spirit, who is in you, whom you have received from God? You

are not your own; you were bought at a price. Therefore honor God with your body.

> "Self-control doesn't mean Self-*IN*-Control."

When a person comes forward in our church, whether to receive Christ or to transfer membership, he or she repeats a confession of faith: "I believe that Jesus is the Christ, the Son of the Living God, my Lord and Savior." We aren't just taking Jesus as Savior. That is the easy part. We are acknowledging Him as Lord. He is the one who has control. When we allow Christ to control our lives through the wisdom of the Scriptures and the guidance of the Holy Spirit, we come under His authority, and He begins to change us.

How is it that a person who once had a violent temper or struggled with alcohol addiction or fought an eating disorder or battled foul language is able to gain control over those emotions or desires? It is not easy, but God makes it possible. Romans 8:9 reminds us, "You, however, are controlled . . . by the Spirit, if the Spirit of God lives in you." I am convinced that is true, but the unfortunate reality is that so many of us refuse to submit to God's authority or the Holy Spirit's presence.

THE DEMAND FOR SELF-CONTROL

Our culture displays an amazing lack of self-control. After an umpire called, "Strike three," a rookie baseball player, in anger and protest, threw his bat high into the air. The umpire quickly said, "Son, if that bat comes down, you are out of the game." Have you ever allowed your emotions to get the best of you, and later regretted it? I remember watching an elementary age church basketball game when I was in middle school. Two dads began arguing in the stands, and before long they were throwing punches. I will never forget one grandma pounding the men with her umbrella as the referees tried to break up the fight. Eventually the police had to be called. I have seen parents out of control at T-Ball games, students out of control at high school football games, coaches out of control on the sidelines. I have seen Christians lose control at church softball games. In the home, infants cry until their little faces turn red, toddlers throw tempter tantrums, young children whine and pout, teenagers yell and slam doors, and parents do all of the above! Even in the church, I have watched men storm out of board meetings, and I have heard arguments over everything from the most obscure points of the by-laws to whether or not a man could be a deacon if he had hair down over his collar. There are a lot of angry people in the world.

And it is not just anger that robs us of control. The desire for revenge, for sex, for wealth; the emotions of envy, bitterness, and discouragement; these passions and others often lead to a loss of control. Proverbs 29:11 specifically says that, "A fool gives full vent to his anger," but it seems to me that we make fools of ourselves when we give full vent to these other emotions as well. That proverb concludes by saying, "But a wise man keeps himself under control."

God commands His people to be self-controlled. In fact, it is such a serious command that a lack of control kept Moses out of the Promised Land. For forty years, Moses led perhaps the most stubborn group of people ever assembled across the wilderness of Palestine, waiting for the day that he could lead them across the Jordan River to take possession of their promised inheritance. However, because Moses angrily struck the rock with his staff after God had

God commands His people to be self-controlled.

instructed him to pray for water to come from it, God refused to allow Moses to enter the land that he longed to inhabit. It was a harsh punishment, but God intended for Moses to realize that His command for self-control is very, very serious.

In Titus chapter 2, Paul makes it clear that self-control is the responsibility of *all* Christians. He tells Titus to teach the older men to be self-controlled, to teach the older women to train the younger women to be self-controlled, and to encourage the young men to be self-controlled. It is a necessity, whether you are nine, twenty-nine or a hundred and nine.

When I was in high school, my English class watched a movie based on the true story of King Henry II of England and Thomas à Becket, the Archbishop of Canterbury. Peter O'Toole played the king who grew up with Becket, played by Richard Burton. The two of them caroused through adolescence into early adulthood, living for wine, women, and song. They were very much out of control. Once Henry became King and began to deal with matters of state, he regularly experienced conflict with the Church of England led by the Archbishop of Canterbury. He came up with the brilliant idea of appointing his chancellor and longtime friend Becket to be the new Archbishop. Thinking Becket would be his puppet, he assumed he would control both church and state.

However, following Becket's promotion, a startling change began to take place. He took his new role very seriously. He became not only religious but godly. He opposed his king and lifelong friend to the point that Henry ultimately had him executed. Thomas à Becket went to the grave, no longer lacking self-control, but living under the control of Almighty God. Self-control is such a pivotal issue in Scripture. The Bible is filled with examples of those who either modeled self-control or completely lacked it. However, no one better demonstrated this final fruit of the Spirit than Jesus Christ.

THE DEMONSTRATION OF SELF-CONTROL

The closing chapters in the Gospel of Matthew record the trials, death, and resurrection of Jesus. These events are often referred to as the "Passion" of Christ because of the intense emotional, physical, and spiritual suffering He endured. Despite the overwhelming trauma, Jesus maintained an incredible sense of self-control, a dramatic climax to a life of willpower and discipline. For three years, Jesus invested His life in Judas Iscariot, one of His twelve closest companions. Yet, on the night before His death, none other than Judas himself showed up in the Garden of Gethsemane to hand Him over to His enemies. Jesus could have exploded in anger, but He maintained His composure. If that were not painful enough, Matthew 26:56b tells us that, "All the disciples deserted him and fled." How do you suppose Jesus must have felt: hurt? angry? disappointed? Except for that moment on the cross when God turned His face away, I doubt Jesus ever felt more alone in His life. He literally did not have a friend in the world.

Following the arrest, He was taken to the palace of the High Priest where He was grilled by the members of the Sanhedrin, the Jewish ruling council. After listening to the testimony of numerous false witnesses, Matthew 26:63b-66 says that the high priest said to him, "I charge you under oath by the living God: Tell us if you are the Christ, the Son of God."

> "Yes, it is as you say," Jesus replied. "But I say to all of you: In the future you will see the Son of Man sitting at the right hand of the Mighty One and coming on the clouds of heaven."

> Then the high priest tore his clothes and said, "He has spoken blasphemy! Why do we need any more witnesses? Look, now you have heard the blasphemy. What do you think?"
>
> "He is worthy of death," they answered.

Imagine, they charged Him with blasphemy, the most horrible of sins, because He told the truth about being the Son of God. His emotions could easily have gone beyond discouragement to anger. If anyone should have supported His ministry, it was these religious leaders, but they refused. And the misery was far from over. Matthew 26:67-68 continues, "They spit in his face and struck him with their fists. Others slapped him and said, 'Prophesy to us, Christ. Who hit you?'" I have read numerous times that Jesus was abused by the soldiers, but Matthew states here that the religious leaders themselves were also punishing Him. Despite the horrible injustice, Jesus refused to retaliate. He accepted their cruel and unjust sentence of death.

It is hard to stay calm when we are angry. The natural response is to lash out, to become abusive with our words or our fists. But Jesus refused to do that.

Still further, when it would have been easy to quit, Jesus maintained control. In Matthew 26:53, He explained that at any time He could call on twelve legions of angels to rescue Him from the crucifixion. That temptation must have been intense considering all He was forced to endure. Who would not have wanted to escape? Yet, Jesus controlled His emotions. He did not perform a miracle to free Himself. He refused to quit, even when they drove spikes through His hands and feet and nailed Him to the cross.

When it would have been easy to quit, Jesus maintained control.

It is human nature to avoid unpleasant circumstances. Paul

Celauro, a handcuffed inmate in Tom's River, New Jersey, saw his window of opportunity as he awaited a court appearance on domestic violence charges. As he was being led down a hallway, he dove through an open, second-story window. Unfortunately for him, he landed unconscious on a judge's Mercedes Benz. Celauro was not hurt in the eight-foot fall, but he was charged with attempted escape. Paul Harvey concluded his report on the story, "I hope he didn't scratch the car or he'll be in for life." Most of us long to escape pain, heartache, and punishment. Jesus had every opportunity to escape the cross. Over in Matthew 27:39-40 we are told, "Those who passed by hurled insults at him, shaking their heads and saying, 'You who are going to destroy the temple and build it in three days, save yourself! Come down from the cross, if you are the Son of God!'" Jesus probably longed to be anywhere but there, doing anything but dying. Yet He stayed right where He was, because as easy as it would have been to quit, He knew this was the purpose for His incarnation. He focused on the goal and maintained self-control. He did the right thing, even though it was incredibly hard.

Jesus probably longed to be anywhere but there, doing anything but dying.

He further demonstrated self-control by avoiding the natural thirst for revenge. The final chapter of Matthew records the account of Christ's resurrection on the first day of the week. Several women came to the tomb to wrap His body in spices, but instead of finding a corpse, they were met by angels. Upon hearing the proclamation that Jesus had risen from the dead, Matthew 28:8-10 tells us,

> The women hurried away from the tomb, afraid yet filled with joy, and ran to tell his disciples. Suddenly Jesus met them.

> "Greetings," he said. They came to him, clasped his feet and worshiped him. Then Jesus said to them, "Do not be afraid. Go and tell my brothers to go to Galilee; there they will see me."

I am amazed that, after the resurrection, Jesus only appeared to His friends. There may have been some skeptics who saw Him after He came back to life, but as far as we know, He did not appear to any of His enemies. That shows incredible restraint. I would have gone immediately to the Sanhedrin! Just pop in to the middle of the meeting and say, "Hey, fellas, I'm back!" Or how about materializing right in the middle of the table where the soldiers were playing a game of poker? "Just came to get My robe!" Or maybe slip into Pilate's bedroom, say, "Ta-da!" and then disappear! I would love to see the look on their faces! But Jesus didn't do that! He did not come to get revenge or scare people half to death. He came to save the world from sin and then empower His followers to proclaim that good news throughout the world. His goal would be accomplished just fine without His taunting His enemies.

Jesus maintained self-control throughout His life to the point of death and far beyond. The challenge for us, then, is to develop a similar level of self-control in our own lives, to echo that control day by day. How can we do that?

THE DEVELOPMENT OF SELF-CONTROL

It was the top of the fifth inning when a Little League Baseball coach confronted one of his players: "Do you understand what it means to play as a team?" Wide-eyed, the little boy nodded. "And do you understand that what matters is not whether we win or lose, but how we play the game?" the coach demanded. The little boy said that he did. "So," the coach continued, "when a strike is called or you're out at first, you don't argue or curse or attack the umpire. Do you understand all that?" Again, the little boy nodded. "Good," the coach said. "Now go over there and explain it to your mother!" Whether it is a mom at a Little League game, a student in the locker room, or a senior adult in a church business meeting, we all need to work on this vital fruit of the Spirit. Here are some quick suggestions.

1. Consider the consequences of a loss of control.

Think for a minute about what people are like when they are out of control. Abusive behavior often results. I am not talking about disciplining children—not even spanking. I am talking about hitting children in a fit of rage, calling names, cursing, physically harming a spouse or parent. How often are relationships damaged, sometimes beyond repair, because one or both parties spew venom in a fit of rage? When we lose control, addictive behavior can develop pretty quickly. Our staff traveled back from a convention one week, and arrived home at about 2:30 Saturday morning. Turning onto our street, we saw a man sitting in his car in the middle of the road with his headlights turned off. As we slowly went around him, he gunned the motor, and swerved back and forth as he accelerated toward us. We shouted for our driver to run the red light, narrowly avoiding being hit by this driver who was obviously drunk. Loss of control led to addictive behavior which produced further loss of control.

When we lose control, we often embarrass ourselves and our family. I once preached a sermon on gentleness during a fruit of the Spirit series. A friend of mine called that evening to

> When we lose control, we often embarrass ourselves and our family.

confess that he was not very gentle with the waitress at the restaurant that afternoon. He did get his meal free because of the poor service, but his ten-year-old daughter said later, "Dad, I've never been scared of you before!" He felt terrible about it!

Can you think of situations you wish you could relive because you lost control and made a fool of yourself? Maybe it was a little thing like being too abrupt in a restaurant. Maybe it was the shame and disgrace of a serious sin like theft or adultery. When we lose control, we are not the only ones who suffer. We often alienate others when we are out of control. If someone hands you a lighted firecracker, you are not going to want to hold it for very long. And if you or I have a short fuse, and we constantly lose our composure, people are not going to want to be around us for very long. You might ask yourself this question: "What if someone were videotaping me at this moment?" It is hard, in the heat of the moment, to think of that. But what if this moment were being preserved for posterity? What if your kids were going to watch the video! How would your lack of control impact their future behavior? I have heard it said, "When a parent lives by a double standard, the child always follows the easier of the two." Your example is incredibly important!

If someone hands you a lighted firecracker, you are not going to want to hold it for very long.

Another helpful question might be, "Is my attitude, at this moment, honoring God?" When Christian people go out onto the basketball court or the softball field and then lose control, shouting at officials and displaying a poor attitude, it completely undermines their Christian witness. At work, if we fall apart every time things don't go our way, or we have a foul mouth when we get frustrated, we are going to lose credibility. If we cannot maintain control, we need to be mature enough to remove ourselves from the situation until we regain our composure.

> If we cannot maintain control, we need to be mature enough to remove ourselves from the situation

I remember several frustrating months that I experienced persistent trouble with my cellular phone bill. The company had changed my home calling area without notifying me about it, and I couldn't get the situation resolved. After calling the Customer Service number a couple of times to fix my bill, I went to the local store to see about clarifying my plan. The woman there was polite, but she wanted to make it clear up front that she had nothing to do with my bill. That was a customer service matter. I explained to her that I had already talked with customer service, but I was not happy about my home service area being changed without being notified. She stressed that she had nothing to do with that either. I stressed that I was not blaming her, but I was not happy and wanted to get the situation resolved.

Now, I'm a preacher. Voice inflection is a part of my job. I may have been a little forceful in making my point, but this was a frustrating situation. In the middle of our conversation, another employee in the store walked out from the back, saw me, and said, "Hey, aren't you a preacher?" That was a low blow! It was totally irrelevant to the conversation! I immediately became more subdued. "Yes, I'm Mark Jones from First Christian Church." She said, "How are you doing?" I smiled and said, "Well, I'm being a pain in the neck at the moment!" We all laughed, the tension was eased, and I was able to get my problem resolved. The truth is, I needed to remember this principle: *We're never persuasive when we're abrasive.* I also needed to remember that people are always watching how we react, especially to frustrating situations. It may be even more critical because I'm a preacher, but every one of us, as Christians, needs to remember that we wear the name of Christ. We echo God's self-control when we respond to people in a Christlike way, especially during frustrating situations.

We're never persuasive when we're abrasive.

2. Learn to constructively vent your emotions.

As our staff drove south toward the Leadership Conference I mentioned earlier, we sat through some serious traffic in Tennessee. At one point, we had been sitting bumper-to-bumper for ten minutes or so without going farther than three or four car-lengths. Bobby Johnson, our Student Minister, was driving when he suddenly noticed the road sign in the median that said, "Reduced Speed Ahead." He said, "Reduced Speed? We couldn't go any slower!" He put the van in park, got out, walked over, and kicked the sign! Then he got back in. It did not fix anything, but he felt better, and several other drivers got a laugh out of it!

Just as a pressure cooker has a safety valve that releases steam so the cooker will not explode, we need to blow off steam and vent emotion to keep from blowing up inwardly or outwardly. If we do not learn to do that, our emotions will eventually explode out of us. When we fail to act wisely, we usually end up reacting offensively. I asked our staff on that trip how they constructively vent their emotions. They listed things like physical exercise, sports, journaling, or eating chocolate! Even crying can be a healthy means of releasing pent-up emotion.

I have a friend who had one room in his house just for his

drum set. Whenever he got uptight, he would go in there, put headphones on and beat the daylights out of those drums. In many ways, that room was his key to sanity. I do not know how his neighbors maintained their sanity, but it helped him! We all need that healthy form of release.

3. Pray persistently for God's strength.

Remember what we said earlier? This fruit may be called "*self*-control," but that does not mean it is all up to us. It is Self-UNDER-Control. This is a fruit of the Spirit, a result of the Holy Spirit's presence in our lives. We cannot control ourselves by ourselves. The only way we can effectively echo God's self-control is to give Jesus Christ control of our lives. Romans 8:6 says, "The mind controlled by the Spirit is life and peace. . . ." We need to pray daily that God would give us the strength of character and the presence of mind to maintain our emotions. And so, we contemplate the consequences of a loss of control. We learn to vent our emotions constructively. We pray for strength. And when we lose control, we confess that to God and go on.

> The only way we can effectively echo God's self-control is to give Jesus Christ control.

NOTES

[1]John Feinstein, "The Punch," *Sports Illustrated* (Oct. 21, 2002): 68-77.

Reflecting on Lesson Nine

1. Can you think of a time when your emotions got the best of you? What happened?

2. How would you explain the difference between self-in-control and self-under-control? Which approach better describes your attempt at controlling yourself?

3. Do you constructively vent your emotions, or do you bottle things up inside? How could you begin to release some of that pressure?

Consider this:

Has this study helped you in your spiritual growth. Do you see any signs of any characteristic of the fruit of the Spirit becoming more a part of your way of life? Are you ready to experience some of the trials which will help God develop these characteristics in you? Are you willing to surrender to His molding? What will help you be willing?

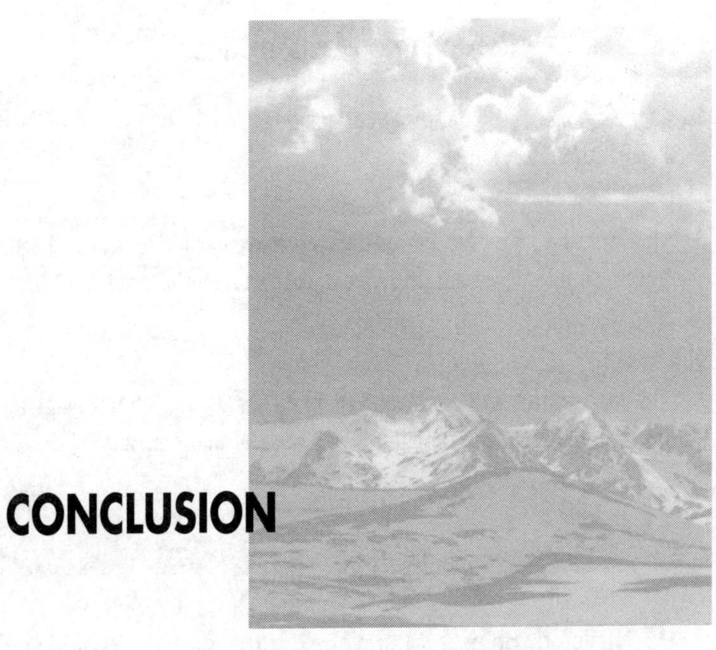

CONCLUSION

Jesus consistently modeled the fruit of the Spirit. He perfectly exemplified godliness. He flawlessly demonstrated the nine key qualities that God's Holy Spirit cultivates in us as Christians. I entitled this book, "Echoes of Heaven," but could have easily called it, *How to Be a Christian*, or *What a Christian Ought to Look Like*.

Now that you have read this book, I would like to think that you have it down pat. These nine traits are firmly in place. You are free to move on to other topics. But it doesn't work that way. Just because these attributes originate from God, that does not mean we will immediately excel in all nine of them the minute we surrender our lives to Christ. God forgives us, cleanses us, and welcomes us into His family immediately upon conversion, but the transformation process goes on for the rest of our lives.

I once heard John Maxwell say, "You can't fax character, and you can't microwave the fruit of the Spirit." All of this takes time. These traits must be cultivated. Remember the imagery we have used throughout this study: An echo requires an original sound just as a reflection requires an original image. We echo these traits that originate from God. We reflect the qualities that Jesus modeled so perfectly.

Sometimes conditions make an echo extremely clear, and sometimes a reflection offers a nearly exact replica of the original. At other times, the echo is weak, the reflection murky. The reality is that some of us echo God's qualities more readily than others. Some of us reflect Christ more precisely. No matter where we are in the process, we all should be growing in these nine critical qualities. The echo should be clearer today than it was a year ago. The reflection should be growing steadily sharper day by day.

Maybe you have heard the saying: "I'm not what I could be; I'm not what I should be; I'm not what I will be. But thank God, I'm not what I was." The Christian life is a process, a journey, and *"the fruit of the Spirit is love, joy, peace, patience, kindness, goodness, faithfulness, gentleness and self-control. Against such things there is no law."*

ABOUT THE AUTHOR

Mark Jones grew up in Louisville, Kentucky, receiving his Bachelor's Degree from Cincinnati Bible College and a Master of Ministry Degree from Kentucky Christian College. Mark preached for three years in Madisonville, Kentucky, and then seven years back in Louisville at Fern Creek Christian Church. He served as the Senior Minister of First Christian Church in Columbus, Indiana, from 1996–2003. Mark has recently partnered with the Savannah Christian Church in Savannah, Georgia, to launch a new church in Bluffton, South Carolina, in the Fall of 2004. He married Gail Foster in 1984, and they have three children: Aaron, Daniel, and MacKenzie. Mark is an avid photographer, providing the photographs for this book. He also enjoys reading, golf, and basketball.